The New Reader

as

Detective

Burton Goodman

AMSCO

AMSCO SCHOOL PUBLICATIONS, INC.
315 Hudson Street, New York, N.Y. 10013

About the Author

Burton Goodman is a former teacher of English. He is the author of more than 70 educational texts and a novel for young adults. Mr. Goodman has written the scripts for numerous children's animated TV shows, including the "Crafts and Culture" segments of *Vegetable Soup* for PBS.

Reviewers:

Stacie Bourgeois, English Teacher
St. Dominic School
New Orleans, LA

Patricia Duskee, Teacher of
    English/Test Prep, I–IV
Williamstown High School
Williamstown, NJ

Stephanie Burke, English Teacher
Lakisha Gilllus-Stith, Lead English Teacher
Hester J. Mallory, Special Education
    English Teacher
James Solomon Russell School
Lawrenceville, VA

Jennifer Raymond, Reading Specialist
Prairie View Middle School
Tinley Park, IL

Dr. Robert L. Hickson, Accountability
    and Support Specialist
Office of Accountability
Department of Education
New York, NY

Peggy Sullivan, English Teacher
D'Iberville Middle School
D'Iberville, MS

Text and Cover Design: Delgado & Company
Cover Illustration of Detective and Dog: Copyright © ImageZoo Illustration/Veer
Composition: Sierra Graphics, Inc.

Please visit our Web site at: *www.amscopub.com*
When ordering this book, please specify:
R 607 P *or* THE NEW READER AS DETECTIVE

ISBN: 978-1-56765-208-6 / *NYC Item: 56765-208-5*

To the Student

The New Reader as Detective has been specially designed to make you a more active reader—to help you become more involved in the reading process.

We believe that a good reader is like a good detective.

Think about this. When you read a powerful story of detection, suspense, mystery, or action, you march along with the characters in search of the ending, or solution. You *are*—or *should* become—the Reader as Detective. Reading is an adventure—one in which you have become *involved*. Furthermore, the greater your involvement, the better reader you will become—and the more you will enjoy and appreciate reading.

This book will help make *you* the Reader as Detective. It does this in a number of ways.

As noted above, the good reader must "march along with the characters in search of the ending, or solution." To encourage you to do this, each story in this volume contains a special and unique feature. It is called "Now it's time for YOU to be the Reader as Detective." This feature usually appears near the conclusion of each story. It provides you with an opportunity to be a reading detective—to guess how the story will end. After a while, you will learn to look for and discover clues and hints that will help you in this task.

A good reader is like a good detective in another way. To succeed, the detective must be able to gain an overall impression of the case, to recognize clues, identify important details, put events in sequence, draw inferences, and distinguish fact from opinion. Similarly, the effective reader must be a *reading* detective—on the search for the main idea, for supporting details, clues, inferences, and so forth. In a word, the reader, like the detective, must *master the skills* necessary to obtain successful results.

This volume provides ample opportunities for you to master these skills. Following each story are 25 short-answer questions. Questions 1 to 10 (**Be a Reading Detective**) offer repeated practice in *the six basic reading skills* essential for achieving reading success. A symbol next to each question identifies the *kind* of reading skill that particular question helps you to develop. Each symbol is related to detection. On the following page are the symbols and the skills they represent.

THE SHERLOCK HOLMES HAT
finding the *main idea*

A MAGNIFYING GLASS
identifying *supporting details*

FINGERPRINTS
finding *vocabulary clues*

A TRAIL OF FOOTPRINTS
putting events in *sequence*

ILLUMINATED LIGHTBULB
drawing *inferences*

DNA STRAND
distinguishing *fact* from *opinion*

Questions 11 to 15 (**Follow the Trail**) help you to track down and understand story elements such as plot, characterization, setting, mood, author's purpose, and text structure.

Questions 16 to 20 (**Find Word Meanings**) help you become a kind of word detective. By using context clues and cloze (sentence completion and sentence context techniques), you will develop vocabulary skills.

Questions 21 to 25 (**Look at Language**) help you understand how words work in a sentence. You'll examine word choice and word relationships, and you'll consider how an author uses descriptive and figurative language to bring a story to life.

A final section (**Review the Case**) offers a wide variety of interesting activities for discussion, writing, and technology use—projects that will help you to review the story and to extend your thinking about what you read.

The first story, "The Adventure of the Speckled Band," introduces the master detective Sherlock Holmes. To help familiarize you with the format of this volume, the story has been divided into three parts. In each part, you will note the *techniques*, or skills, that Holmes uses to solve the case. You will be encouraged to use similar techniques as you read.

There are 22 reading selections in this volume. The stories, and the exercises that follow them, are intended to help you develop an *active, participatory* approach to reading. They can help you develop a very special kind of reading habit—one that will serve you for a lifetime. Now, let's begin. It's time for you to become the Reader as Detective!

Burton Goodman

Contents

Her face was pale, with restless, frightened eyes, like those of some hunted animal.

The Adventure of the Speckled Band

PART I

by Sir Arthur Conan Doyle

For the past eight years, I have studied more than 70 cases solved by my good friend, Sherlock Holmes. Some of them were funny. Others were quite strange. But not one was ordinary. Of his many cases, however, I can think of none more unusual than "The Adventure of the Speckled Band."

It began early in April in the year of 1883. I was sharing rooms with Holmes on Baker Street in those days. A sudden noise awoke me one morning. I looked up to find Sherlock Holmes standing, fully dressed, by the side of the bed. The clock showed that it was just a quarter past seven.

"Very sorry to wake you up, Watson," said Holmes. "I was awakened early myself."

"What is it, then? A fire?"

"No, it seems a young lady has arrived. She is very upset. She insisted upon seeing me and is now waiting in the sitting room."

I looked at Holmes with growing interest.

"I can tell you this, Watson," he continued, "when young ladies wander about the city at this hour of the morning, when they get sleepy people out of their beds, they must have something important to say. This may prove to be an interesting case, Watson. You may wish to follow it from the start. I thought I should wake you and give you that chance."

"My dear fellow, I would not miss it for anything."

I quickly put on my clothes. In minutes I was ready to accompany my friend to the sitting room. A lady dressed in black rose as we entered.

"Good morning, madam," said Holmes cheerfully. "My name is Sherlock Holmes. This is my good friend and companion, Dr. Watson. You may speak as freely before him as before me."

Holmes glanced across the room to the fireplace. "I am glad to see such a roaring fire," he said. "Please pull your chair up to it, for I observe that you are shivering."

"It is not the cold which makes me shiver," the woman said in a low voice.

"What is it then?"

"It is fear, Mr. Holmes. It is terror."

She raised her veil as she spoke, and we could see that her words were true. Her face was pale, with restless, frightened eyes, like those of some hunted animal.

Holmes bent forward. "You must not fear," he said soothingly. "We shall, I am sure, soon set matters right. You have, I see, come in by train this morning."

She looked at him with surprise. "Do you know me, then?"

"No, but I observe the second half of a return ticket in the palm of your left glove. You must have started early. Yet you had a long drive in a cart, along muddy roads, before you reached the station."

The lady stared in surprise at my companion.

"It is no mystery," said Holmes, smiling. "The left arm of your jacket is splattered with mud. The marks are quite fresh. No vehicle but a cart throws up mud that way—and then only when you sit on the left-hand side of the driver."

"Whatever your reasoning may be, you are perfectly correct."

The lady suddenly sat up straight in her chair. "Mr. Holmes," she said, "I have heard of you. Perhaps you can help me. Perhaps you can throw a little light on the darkness that surrounds me."

She paused. "At the moment I cannot pay you for your services. But in a month or six weeks I shall be married and shall have my own money. I can pay you then."

"I can only say, madam," replied Holmes, "that I shall be happy to take your case. You may pay me when it pleases you. Now tell us everything that may help us."

"My name is Helen Stoner," she said. "I live with my stepfather. He is the last of the Roylotts of Stoke Moran, a famous family in England."

Holmes nodded his head. "The Roylotts," he said. "I have heard the name."

"Once," she said, "the family was rich and their lands stretched far. Little, however, is left today. A small piece of land and a very old house are all that remain.

"My stepfather became a doctor," said Miss Stoner. "He went to India. It was in India that Dr. Roylott married my mother. My father had died when my twin sister Julia and I were only two years old. Soon after, my mother was killed in a railroad accident. She was very wealthy and left all her money to Dr. Roylott. But the will stated that a certain sum of money would be given to each of us when we married."

"And how large a sum was that?" asked Holmes.

"That I do not know," replied Miss Stoner. "But I believe it may be considerable."

"I see," said Holmes.

"Dr. Roylott then left India. My sister and I went to live with him in the old house at Stoke Moran."

Helen Stoner shook her head sadly. "At Stoke Moran our stepfather changed completely. He shut himself up in the old house. He seldom went out. When he did venture forth, he fought with whoever happened to cross his path. As you can imagine, he was not very popular. People ran from him when he came near, for he is a man of very great strength.

"He has no friends at all, Mr. Holmes— except for a few wandering vagabonds. He lets them stay on his land. But he does love animals from India. They are sent to him from that country. He has a cheetah and a baboon, which roam freely over the grounds. The villagers are almost as afraid of the animals as they are of my stepfather.

"You can guess that my poor sister Julia and I did not have much pleasure in our lives. She was only thirty at the time of her death. Yet her hair was already turning white."

"Your sister is dead, then?" said Holmes.

"She died two years ago. It is because of her death that I came to speak to you.

"Two years ago, at Christmas, we were visiting a relative near London. There Julia met a man who wanted to marry her. My step-father agreed. But two weeks before the wedding something terrible happened."

Sherlock Holmes looked closely at his visitor. "Please," he said, "explain exactly what occurred."

"I can do that easily," said Miss Stoner, "for I shall never forget that fatal day. As I have told you, the house is very old. Only three bedrooms are now in use. They are all on the ground floor. The first is my own, the second my sister's, and the third Dr. Roylott's. The bedrooms are all side by side, though there are no doors between them. But they all open out to the same hall. Am I making myself clear?"

"Perfectly."

"The windows of the three rooms look out upon the garden. That fatal night, Dr. Roylott had gone to bed early. He was not yet asleep, however. My sister was bothered by the smell of the Indian cigars which he likes to smoke. She, therefore, left her room and came into mine. We sat there chatting.

"'Tell me, Helen,' she said, 'have you ever heard anyone whistling in the middle of the night?'

"'Never,' said I.

"'Is it possible that you whistle in your sleep?'

"'Certainly not. But why?'

"'For the last few nights,' said she, 'I have been awakened by a low, clear whistle. I cannot tell where it came from—perhaps from the room, perhaps from the garden. I thought that I would ask you if you had heard it.'

"'No,' I answered. 'It is probably the vagabonds on the grounds.'

"'Very likely. Yet I'm surprised that you didn't hear it, too.'

"'Ah, but I sleep more heavily than you.'

"'Well, it doesn't matter.' She smiled at me and closed the door. A few moments later, I heard the key turn in her lock."

"Indeed," said Holmes. "Did you always lock your doors at night?"

"Always."

"And why?"

"I think that I mentioned to you that Dr. Roylott had a cheetah and a baboon. We did not feel safe unless our doors were locked."

"Quite so. Please go on." said Holmes.

"I could not sleep that night. A storm raged. Outside, the wind was howling, and the rain beat against the windows. Suddenly, in the middle of the gale, I heard the wild screams of a terrified woman. I knew at once that it was my sister's voice.

"I jumped from the bed and rushed into the hall. As I opened my door, I seemed to hear a low whistle. Then I heard a clanging sound, as if something made of metal had fallen. As I ran down the hall, I saw my sister's door open. By the light of the lamp, I saw my sister at the opening. Her face was white with terror.

"I ran to her and threw my arms around her. But her knees seemed to give way and she fell to the ground. Then she screamed, in a voice which I shall never forget. 'Helen! It was the band! The speckled band!' She pointed in the direction of the doctor's room but could say no more.

"I rushed out, calling loudly for my stepfather. I met him hurrying from his room. But, by the time he reached my sister's side, she had already died. Such was the dreadful end of my beloved sister."

"One moment," said Holmes. "Are you sure about the whistle and the sound of metal that followed?"

"I believe so," said Miss Stoner. "And yet, I cannot say so with confidence. With the noise of the storm, I may have been mistaken."

"Did the police investigate?" asked Holmes.

"Very carefully. But they could not find the cause of my sister's death. Her door had been locked from the inside, and the shutter of her window was locked with a strong iron bar. The walls and the floor were also found to be solid. It is certain, therefore, that Julia was alone when she met her end. Furthermore," continued Miss Stoner, "there were no marks of any kind on her."

"What about the possibility of poison?" asked Holmes.

"The doctor found no sign of it."

Holmes thought for a moment. "What do you think your sister died of?" he asked.

"It is my belief that she died of shock," said Miss Stoner. "Though what it was that frightened her I cannot imagine."

"And what," asked Holmes, "did she mean by 'the band. The speckled band'?"

"I do not know. It may refer to a band of people—vagabonds who camp on our land. Many of them wear spotted—speckled—handkerchiefs over their heads."

Holmes shook his head and looked doubtful. "Please go on with your story," he said.

"Two years have passed since then. My life has been lonelier than ever until lately. A month ago, a dear friend whom I have known for years asked me to marry him. My stepfather has agreed and we are to be married in the spring. Two days ago some repairs were started in the house. I had to move into the bedroom in which my sister died, to sleep in her bed.

"Imagine then my terror when I suddenly awoke, and heard, in the silence of the night, the low whistle my sister had described. I jumped up and turned on the lamp. There was nothing in the room. I was too upset to go back to bed, however. I dressed, and left the house as soon as it was daylight. I decided to come here to ask your help."

"You have acted wisely," said Holmes. "We must move quickly. There is not a moment to lose. We must leave at once for Stoke Moran!"

Now it's time for YOU to be the Reader as Detective.

The following exercises will help you accomplish this. Like Sherlock Holmes, you will learn to look for clues, find details, put events in sequence, and so forth. You will also learn to anticipate, or think ahead.

Be a Reading Detective

Read each of the following questions. Then write the letter of the correct answer to each question. Remember, the symbol next to each question identifies the *kind* of reading skill that particular question helps you to develop.

Let's review the symbols.

finding the *main idea*

 identifying *supporting details*

 finding *vocabulary clues*

 putting events in *sequence*

 drawing *inferences*

 distinguishing *fact* from *opinion*

 1. Holmes woke Watson because
   a. Holmes wanted to leave for his office.
   b. it was already a quarter past seven.
   c. a new client had arrived.
   d. he woke Watson every day at 7:15.

 2. Helen Stoner was shivering because she was
   a. ill.
   b. frightened.
   c. cold.
   d. shy.

3. Holmes observed fresh marks on his visitor's jacket. As used in this sentence, what is the meaning of the word *fresh*?

a. outspoken
b. untried
c. new
d. ugly

4. Which happened last?

a. Julia Stoner died.
b. Dr. Roylott went to India.
c. Helen Stoner moved into her sister's bedroom.
d. Holmes took on the case.

5. You can infer that Watson followed Holmes's cases

a. with great interest.
b. with little interest.
c. now and then.
d. only on special occasions.

6. " 'He shut himself up in the old house. He seldom went out. When he did venture forth, he fought with whoever happened to cross his path.' " Which word or expression BEST defines the word *seldom* as used here?

a. never
b. rarely
c. often
d. always

7. Which expression BEST describes the night on which Julia Stoner died?

a. calm and peaceful
b. wild and stormy
c. bright and sunny
d. hot and clammy

8. At the end of this part of the story, Helen Stoner probably felt
   a. sorrowful.
   b. ill.
   c. relieved.
   d. surprised.

9. Which statement expresses an opinion?
   a. The case began in April.
   b. The Roylott family was once very wealthy.
   c. It was certain that Holmes would solve the case.
   d. Helen Stoner is a twin.

10. Which is the BEST subtitle for this part of the story?
    a. A Strange Case Begins
    b. I Hate Working Early
    c. Truth Is Stranger Than Fiction
    d. Solving a Difficult Case

Follow the Trail

Story Clues

How well do you spot story clues? **Story clues** are hints or signposts that point the way to how the story will end. As you read, learn to look for and to recognize story signs.

Each of the following questions is based on a story clue found in the selection. The correct answers play an important part in the story. They can help you solve the mystery of "the Speckled Band."

11. Mrs. Stoner's will stated that each daughter would
    a. receive a certain sum of money after getting married.
    b. receive a small piece of land.
    c. share the family's riches with their stepfather.
    d. live with their stepfather if she died.

12. Which statement is true of Dr. Roylott?

   a. He often visited relatives.
   b. He received animals from India.
   c. He was admired by his neighbors.
   d. He had only one friend.

13. Julia Stoner died

   a. in a railroad accident.
   b. two weeks before her marriage.
   c. a month after her wedding.
   d. while she was asleep.

14. On the night of her sister's death, Helen Stoner heard

   a. a low whistle and a clanging sound.
   b. something banging against the door.
   c. vagabonds shouting in the garden.
   d. the cheetah prowling outside.

15. Because of repairs in the house, Helen had to sleep

   a. at an inn.
   b. in a tent on the grounds.
   c. in her sister's bed.
   d. on a different floor.

Review your answers to the questions above. Keep these story clues in mind when you read Part 2 of the story. As you continue to read, look for other story clues. You are on your way to becoming a better reader—and mystery solver.

Find Word Meanings

The five words listed on the next page appear in Part 1 of "The Adventure of the Speckled Band." Study the words and their definitions. Use the page numbers to check how the words are used in the story. Then complete the following sentences by using each vocabulary word only *once*.

word	meaning	page
companion	one who shares in what another is doing	2
soothingly	calmly; quietly	2
observe	see and note; study	2
vehicle	any means of carrying, communicating, or making known	2
fatal	causing death or ruin	4

It's fun to study or _____16_____ Sherlock Holmes at work. No matter how difficult the case appears to be, he approaches it with confidence. He carefully searches for clues that will prove _____17_____ to those who are guilty. Then the master detective very calmly and _____18_____ explains how he solved the mystery.

Dr. Watson serves as the _____19_____ for communicating the tales of Sherlock Holmes. Each adventure is described by Dr. Watson. He's Holmes's friend and _____20_____ .

Look at Language

Nouns

Nouns are words that name people, places, and things. Some examples of nouns are *detective*, *police*, *officer*, *crime scene*, *DNA*, and *fingerprints*. In "The Adventure of the Speckled Band," many of the clues to the mystery involve nouns.

Answer the following questions about the nouns that appeared in the first part of this story.

21 . Which noun tells exactly where the lady waited for Holmes and Watson?

   a. Baker Street
   b. the fireplace
   c. the sitting room
   d. a cart

22. Choose the list of nouns in the following sentence from the story:

   "But the will stated that a certain sum of money would be given to each of us when we married."

   a. stated, would, when
   b. each, certain, married
   c. will, sum, money
   d. but, that, given

23. Below are four pairs of words from the selection. Which contains only nouns?

   a. stepfather, happened
   b. roam, afraid
   c. except, vagabonds
   d. India, Stoke Moran

24. Which words below are nouns that describe possible clues to what happened at Stoke Moran?

   a. face, door
   b. whistle, band
   c. hair, visitor
   d. people, friends

25. A proper noun is the name of a specific place or a person. Which of these is *not* a proper noun?

   a. sister
   b. Roylotts
   c. Stoke Moran
   d. Dr. Watson

Review the Case

The following activities will help you review and reflect on what happened in "The Adventure of the Speckled Band," Part 1.

1. **Discuss.** Reread the last paragraph of the story. Give your reasons for Holmes's statement.

2. **Write.** Imagine if Watson were not present when Miss Stoner gave the details of the case. Prepare a dossier (case file) outlining the facts so far, to help Watson learn about the case. Your case file should be a numbered list of each fact in the case.

3. **Technology Application.** Sir Arthur Conan Doyle, the author, and his character Sherlock Holmes are famous the world over. Conduct research online about either the writer or his character, Sherlock Holmes. Write a one-paragraph biography of the person you chose. If you write about the author, your biography should contain an overview of his life and works. If you write about the character, your biography should describe his most famous personality traits and cases. At the end of your paragraph, list the sources you used.

Dr. Roylott stepped swiftly to the fireplace. He seized the poker and bent it into a curve with his powerful hands. "See that you stay out of my way!" he snarled.

The Adventure of the Speckled Band

PART 2

"Yes," continued Holmes, "we have not a moment to lose. If we were to come to Stoke Moran today, could we see the rooms without your stepfather's knowing it?"

"As it happens," said Miss Stoner, "he spoke of coming to London today on business. He will probably be away all day, so you could look around undisturbed. We have a housekeeper now, but I can easily get her out of the way."

"Excellent. Do you mind making the trip, Watson?"

"No, not at all."

"Then we shall both come."

Holmes turned to his visitor. "When do you plan on returning?" he asked.

"I have one or two things which I would like to do in town. But I shall return by the twelve o'clock train to be there when you arrive."

"You may expect us in the afternoon. I, too, have some matters to attend to. But will you have some breakfast first?"

"No, I must go. But my heart is much lighter now that I have spoken to you. I look forward to seeing you again this afternoon."

With that, Miss Stoner dropped the black veil over her face, and left the room.

Sherlock Holmes leaned back in his chair. "And what do you think of it all, Watson?" he inquired.

"It seems to me a dark and evil business."

"Dark enough and evil enough."

"But if the door and windows were locked, and the floor and walls were solid, then the lady must surely have been alone when she met her mysterious end."

"What, then, of those whistles in the night?" said Holmes. "And what of the strange words of the dying woman?"

"I cannot imagine."

"To find the answers, we are going to Stoke Moran today. I want to see—but what in the name of the devil!"

Our door had suddenly been thrown open and a huge figure of a man stood framed in the doorway. He was wearing a black top hat and a long, dark coat. So tall was he that his hat actually brushed against the top of the doorway. His large face was covered with a heavy dark beard and his eyes blazed at us with hatred.

"Which one of you is Holmes?" asked the figure.

"That is my name, sir. But you have the advantage over me," said my companion softly.

"I am Dr. Grimesby Roylott of Stoke Moran."

"Indeed, Doctor," said Holmes. "Please take a seat."

"I will do nothing of the kind. My stepdaughter has been here. I have traced her. What has she been saying to you?"

"That I cannot tell you," said Holmes.

"What has she been telling you!" shouted the man furiously.

"It is a little cold for this time of year," said Holmes.

"Ha! You put me off, do you?" said our visitor, taking a step forward and shaking his fist. "I know you, you mischief maker! I have heard of you before. You are Holmes, the meddler!"

My friend smiled.

"Holmes, the busybody!"

His smile grew wider.

"Holmes, the nuisance!"

Holmes chuckled loudly. "Your conversation is most amusing," said he. "On your way out, please close the door for I feel a draft."

"I will go when I have said my say. Don't you dare to become involved in my affairs, Mr. Holmes! I know that Miss Stoner has been here. I traced her! I am a dangerous man to fool with. See here!"

Dr. Roylott stepped swiftly to the fireplace. He seized the poker and bent it into a curve with his powerful hands.

"See that you stay out of my way!" he snarled. Then, hurling the twisted poker into the fireplace, Dr. Roylott marched out of the room.

"He does not seem a very friendly person," said Holmes. "I am not quite so large as he, but if he had remained, I might have shown him that my grip is not much weaker than his own." As Holmes spoke, he picked up the steel poker, and with a sudden twist, straightened it out again.

"And now, Watson," said Holmes, "we shall order breakfast. And afterward I hope to obtain some information which may help us greatly. Then we must be on our way to Stoke Moran."

———————◆———————

It was a perfect day. The sun was bright and a few fluffy white clouds hung in the sky. The trees and flowers were showing their first green shoots. The air was filled with the rich smell of the earth. Holmes had hired a cab, and we were on our way to Stoke Moran.

For much of the journey, my friend had been sitting quietly. His arms were folded and his hat was pulled down over his eyes. He seemed to be buried in the deepest of thought. Suddenly Holmes spoke.

"I have seen Mrs. Stoner's will," he said.

"Her daughter spoke of it."

"Yes," said Holmes. "The will states that each of Mrs. Stoner's daughters is to receive a large sum of money on the day that she marries."

"Who is in possession of the money now?"

"Dr. Roylott. This proves, without a doubt, that he had very strong reasons for preventing them from marrying."

The driver suddenly interrupted. "Look there," said he, pointing over the meadows. On the top of a heavily wooded piece of land stood a very old mansion.

"Stoke Moran?" said Holmes.

"Yes, sir. That is the house of Dr. Grimesby Roylott."

"That is where we are going," remarked Holmes.

"There's the village just to the left," said the driver. "But if you want to get to the house, the quickest way is to hop over that wall and take the footpaths through the fields."

"We will do as you suggest," said Holmes.

We got out, paid our fare, and the cab rattled back on its way.

Minutes later, we were greeted at the door by Miss Stoner, who had seen us through a window.

"I have been waiting for you eagerly," she said, shaking hands with us warmly. "All has turned out splendidly. Dr. Roylott has gone to London. He will probably not be back before evening."

"We have had the pleasure of meeting the doctor," said Holmes. And in a few words, he explained what had happened.

"He has followed me then," said Miss Stoner.

"So it appears," replied Holmes. "We must see to it that you are safe from him tonight. But for now, we must make the best use of our time. Kindly take us to the rooms we are to examine."

Miss Stoner led us through the building to the three rooms she had spoken of earlier. They stood side by side. We stepped into the first.

"This, I take it," said Holmes, "is your room. The center one must be your sister's, and the last one, Dr. Roylott's."

"Exactly. But I am sleeping in the middle one now."

"Because of the repairs, as I understand."

"Yes," said Miss Stoner. "But I believe that was just an excuse to get me out of my room and into my sister's room."

Holmes looked around the room. "Ah, that is interesting," he said as he moved to the window. The shutters in front of it were solid and held in place by a strong iron bar. "Hmm," said Holmes, "no one could have gotten in this way if the shutters were locked. Yet, since you both locked your doors, no one could enter from that direction either."

We moved down the hall into the second room—the one in which Miss Stoner now slept. It was the room in which her sister had met her sad fate. It was a gloomy little room with a low ceiling and a large fireplace. A brown chest of drawers stood in one corner, a narrow bed in the other. There was a dressing table along with two small chairs. These made up all the furniture in the room.

Holmes pulled one of the chairs into a corner and sat silently. His eyes traveled round and round, up and down, taking in every detail of the apartment. At last, he pointed to a thick bell rope which hung down near the bed. The end of it was actually lying on the pillow.

"That bell rope," he asked, "where does it go?"

"It goes to the housekeeper's room," said Miss Stoner. "It can be used to ring for her."

"I see. It looks newer than the other things in the room."

"Yes, it was put there only two years ago."

"Your sister asked for it, I suppose," said Holmes.

"No, my sister was very active. I never heard her use it to ring for anything. We always got what we wanted for ourselves."

"Indeed. Then it hardly seems necessary to have put a bell there."

From his pocket, Holmes drew a magnifying glass. "You will excuse me for a few minutes," he said, "while I satisfy myself about this floor." He threw himself down upon his face and crawled swiftly backward and forward, carefully examining the cracks between the boards. Then he did the same with the woodwork on the walls.

"The floor and walls are sound," said Holmes, walking over to the bed. He spent some time staring at it. Then he ran his eyes up and down the wall. Finally, he took the bell rope in his hand and briskly gave it a pull.

There was no sound.

"Why, it's a dummy," said Holmes.

"Won't it ring?"

"No, the bell is not even attached at the top. This is very interesting," said Holmes. "If you look very carefully, you can see that the rope is tied to a hook just above where the little opening of the air ventilator is."

"I never noticed that before," said Miss Stoner.

"Strange," said Holmes. "What a fool the builder was to put an air ventilator between two rooms. With a little more trouble, he might have built it so that it would reach the fresh air outside."

"The ventilator is also quite modern," said Miss Stoner.

"Done about the same time as the bell rope?" remarked Holmes.

"Yes, there were several little changes made about that time."

"That is something to reflect about," said Holmes. "And now, Miss Stoner, with your permission, let us look at Dr. Roylott's room."

Dr. Grimesby Roylott's room was larger than the other two. However, it was furnished as simply. It contained a bed, a shelf full of books, and a large iron safe. A plain wooden chair rested against a wall.

Holmes examined each object carefully. "What's in here?" he asked, tapping the safe.

"My stepfather's business papers."

"There isn't a cat in it, for example."

"Why, no. What a funny idea."

"Well, look at this," said Holmes. He pointed to a small saucer of milk which stood on top of the safe.

"No, we don't have a cat. But there are a cheetah and a baboon."

"Ah, yes, of course. Well, you might consider a cheetah just a big cat. Still, I should think, a saucer of milk won't go very far in satisfying its hunger."

Holmes bent down in front of the wooden chair. "There is one point," he muttered to himself, "about which I should like to be quite positive." He carefully examined the seat of the chair. "Thank you," he said, after a while. "That is quite settled." He returned the magnifying glass to his pocket.

"Hello," said Holmes. "Here is something interesting." The object which had caught his attention was a small dog leash which lay on one corner of the bed. The leash, however, was curled up and tied at the end so that it made a small, tight loop.

"What do you make of that, Watson?"

"It's a common enough dog leash. But I don't know why it should be looped at the end."

"That is not quite so common, is it?" said Holmes. "Ah me, it's a wicked world. And when a clever man turns his head to crime, it's the worst of all. I think that I have seen enough, Miss Stoner."

My friend's face had turned grim. "It is very important, Miss Stoner," said he, "that you follow my advice carefully. Your very life may depend on it."

Miss Stoner and I gazed at Holmes in astonishment. He walked to the window, unlocked the shutters, and looked out. "I believe," said Holmes, "that is the village inn over there."

"Yes," said Miss Stoner. "It is known as the Crown."

"Very good," said Holmes. "And would it be possible to see the window of your room from there?"

"Of course."

"Excellent," said Holmes. "That is where Dr. Watson and I will wait. Now, Miss Stoner, you must lock yourself in your room when your stepfather comes home. Do not see him at all. Then, when you hear him go to bed for the night, you must open the shutters of your window. Place a lighted lamp in the window. That will be the signal to us in the Crown. Quickly, then, go back to the room you used to sleep in. I believe that, in spite of the repairs, you could manage there for one night."

"Oh, yes," said Miss Stoner. "Easily."

"Leave the rest in our hands."

"But what will you do?"

"We shall spend the night in your room. There we shall continue our investigation of the noise that has disturbed you."

"I believe that you have already made up your mind about what it was," said Miss Stoner.

"Yes," said Holmes. "But I would prefer to have some proof before I speak."

"Tell me, at least," said Miss Stoner, "if you believe my sister died of fright."

"No, I do not think so," said Holmes. "I believe there was another cause. But for now, Miss Stoner, we must leave you. If our plan works, we shall soon have all the proof we need."

Now it's time for YOU to be the Reader as Detective.

 Can you figure out how Julia Stoner died? State your best guess. In Part 3, you'll see if you were right!

Be a Reading Detective

Read each of the following questions. Then write the letter of the correct answer to each question. Remember, the symbol next to each question identifies the *kind* of reading skill that particular question helps you to develop.

1. Dr. Roylott was wearing
   a. a brown top hat.
   b. a black sweater.
   c. a long, dark coat.
   d. a silver watch chain.

2. "All has turned out splendidly," said Helen Stoner happily. What is the meaning of the word *splendidly*?
   a. very well
   b. very poorly
   c. very suddenly
   d. very unexpectedly

3. Holmes carefully examined the woodwork on the walls because

a. wood carving was his hobby.

b. he was looking for bloodstains.

c. he wanted to see if anyone could have come in that way.

d. he wanted to see what repairs had been made.

4. Which happened first?

a. Holmes and Watson took a cab to Stoke Moran.

b. Holmes examined the chair with a magnifying glass.

c. Holmes decided to rent a room at the village inn.

d. Holmes said Julia Stoner did not die of fright.

5. Holmes told Helen Stoner to

a. say hello to her stepfather as soon as he returned.

b. lock herself in her room when her stepfather came home.

c. spend the night at the Crown.

d. extinguish her lamp when she went to bed.

6. Which statement expresses a fact?

a. The shutters were held in place by a strong bar.

b. Dr. Roylott was probably hiding somewhere in the house.

c. Holmes believed that Julia Stoner died of fright.

d. A cheetah is a strange pet to keep.

7. In all, how many rooms did Holmes examine?

a. two rooms

b. three rooms

c. four rooms

d. one room

8. You can infer that
   a. Miss Stoner was in great danger.
   b. Holmes was in no hurry to visit Stoke Moran.
   c. Watson had already solved the mystery.
   d. Grimesby Roylott did not stay in town all day.

9. Holmes told Dr. Roylott, "On your way out, please close the door for I feel a *draft*."

   Which BEST defines the word *draft* as used in this sentence?
   a. rough copy
   b. plan or sketch
   c. current of air
   d. cold drink

10. Which sentence BEST expresses the main idea of the selection?
    a. All of the rooms were furnished very simply.
    b. Holmes looked for clues and thought of a plan.
    c. Dr. Roylott bent a poker and hurled it into the fireplace.
    d. Watson was puzzled by the mystery.

Follow the Trail

Story Clues

How well did you spot story clues in this selection? Each of the following questions is based on a story clue found in Part 2 of the story. Each correct answer will help you solve the mystery of "the Speckled Band."

11. Where was the bell rope located?
    a. over the bed
    b. by the window
    c. on the chest of drawers
    d. over the doorway

12. Holmes discovered that the bell rope

    a. was as old as the house.

    b. did not ring.

    c. worked perfectly.

    d. called the housekeeper.

13. What was surprising about the ventilator?

    a. It was between two rooms.

    b. It reached the fresh air outside.

    c. It was very noisy.

    d. It was quite old.

14. What did Holmes find on top of the safe?

    a. some business papers

    b. a saucer of milk

    c. a large cat

    d. a dog leash

15. What was unusual about the dog leash?

    a. It was long and brightly colored.

    b. It was locked in the safe.

    c. It was tied at the end in a small, tight loop.

    d. It was stained with milk.

Review your answers to the questions above. Keep these story clues in mind when you read the conclusion, or ending, to the story. You should be getting closer to solving the mystery.

Find Word Meanings

The five words listed on the next page appear in Part 2 of "The Adventure of the Speckled Band." Study the words and their definitions. Use the page numbers to check how the words are used in the story. Then complete the following sentences by using each vocabulary word only *once*.

word	meaning	page
active	lively; showing much attention	18
reflect	think carefully	19
furnished	supplied	19
satisfying	pleasing; fulfilling	19
investigation	a careful search	20

To be a good reader, you must take an _____16_____ part in the reading adventure. Learn to look for the story clues that the author has supplied, or _____17_____ . Think carefully about each new detail in the story.

Reading, like detective work, requires _____18_____ . Therefore, as you read, make it a habit to reason; to think and _____19_____ . Become more involved in what you are reading.

If you follow this advice, you will become a better reader. You will also find reading much more _____20_____ .

Look at Language

Adjectives

Writers use powerful adjectives to bring the scene to life. As you know, an **adjective** is a word that describes a noun. Some examples of adjectives are *quiet*, *frightening*, *gigantic*, and *calm*. Notice how these powerful adjectives help to create a picture or produce an effect.

Answer the following questions about adjectives. Each one refers to the second part of "The Adventure of the Speckled Band." Now you're looking at language!

21 . Identify the adjective in the following sentence:

"With that, Miss Stoner dropped the black veil over her face, and left the room."

a. that
b. black
c. face
d. left

22. Which italicized word is an adjective?

    a. " 'To find the *answers*, we are going to Stoke Moran today.' "

    b. "For much of the journey, my friend had been sitting *quietly*."

    c. "He seized the poker and bent it into a curve with his *powerful* hands."

    d. "We got out, *paid* our fare, and the cab rattled back on its way."

23. Which adjective BEST describes how Miss Stoner seemed when she first came in to see Holmes?

    a. sneaky
    b. terrified
    c. calm
    d. depressed

24. After Holmes examined the woodwork in Julia Stoner's room, he said, "The floor and walls are sound." What does *sound* mean here?

    a. makes noise when it is tapped
    b. you can hear through the walls
    c. solid
    d. you cannot hear through the walls

25. Which adjective BEST describes Sherlock Holmes?

    a. energetic
    b. annoying
    c. unhappy
    d. clever

Review the Case

The following activities will help you review and reflect on what happened in "The Adventure of the Speckled Band," Part 2.

1. **Discuss.** Draw a sketch of the room in which Julia died. Include all the items described in the story. Then share and discuss your sketch with your classmates. What did Holmes find in the room that might be suspicious or that might lead to solving the case?

2. Write. At the end of the selection, Holmes states that he has a plan in mind. Make up a plan of your own for the case, and write it down in two to three paragraphs. Later, you will have an opportunity to share you answer with your classmates. It will be interesting to see whose plan comes closest to the one Holmes decided upon.

3. Technology Application. If Holmes lived in today's technological world, he might have an anonymous online message board where his fans could follow his cases. Write five brief messages (25–50 words each) that Holmes might have posted about the case so far.

**Suddenly, the silence of the night was broken
by a horrible scream. It was a hoarse yell
filled with anger, pain, and fear.**

The Adventure of the Speckled Band

PART 3

olmes and I had no trouble getting a room at the Crown Inn. It was on the top floor, and from our window we could easily see the old house at Stoke Moran. At dusk, we saw Dr. Grimesby Roylott drive up to the old house and open the door.

Holmes and I sat together waiting in the gathering darkness. "Do you know," he said after a while, "I really am quite concerned about your coming with me tonight. There may be some danger."

"Can I be of help?"

"Your assistance would be of the greatest value."

"Then I shall certainly come."

"That is very kind of you."

"You speak of danger, Holmes. Undoubtedly, you have seen more in those rooms than I did."

"No, but I believe I may have detected a little more."

"I saw nothing unusual except the bell rope. But what purpose that was for, I confess, I cannot imagine."

"You saw the ventilator, too," said Holmes.

"Yes, but I did not think it unusual to have a small opening between two rooms. It was so small that a rat could hardly pass through it."

"I knew that we should find a ventilator before we ever came to Stoke Moran."

"And how could you know that, Holmes?"

"You will remember that Miss Stoner's sister said she could smell Dr. Roylott's cigar. That suggested to me that there must be a common opening between the rooms. A ventilator came immediately to mind."

"But what importance can there be in that?"

"It is very curious, Watson. A ventilator is made, a bell cord is hung, and a lady who sleeps in the bed near them dies. Does anything strike you about that?"

"At the moment, I cannot see any connection."

"Did you observe anything peculiar about that bed?"

"No."

"It was nailed to the floor. Did you ever see a bed fastened like that before?"

"I cannot say that I have."

"The lady could not move her bed. It must therefore always be near the ventilator and the rope. I call it a rope for, clearly, it was never meant to be a bellpull."

"Holmes!" I cried. "I begin to see what you are hinting at. We are just in time to prevent another horrible crime!"

Now it's time for YOU to be the Reader as Detective.

You have all the clues necessary for you to solve "The Adventure of the Speckled Band." Can you figure out how Julia Stoner was murdered? Here are the clues:

- The dummy bell rope
- The ventilator

- The bed nailed to the floor
- The whistling sound
- The clanging sound
- Julia Stoner's dying words
- The saucer of milk
- The safe
- The dog leash
- Dr. Roylott's love of animals from India

Read on to see if you are right!

At that moment, the lights in the old house at Stoke Moran went out and all was dark. Two hours passed slowly. Then, suddenly, at the stroke of eleven, a single bright light shone out from the house.

"That is our signal!" exclaimed Holmes. "It is coming from the middle window."

A moment later, we were on the dark road heading toward the house. We had just slipped into the garden and were about to enter through the window. Suddenly, from out of a clump of bushes, there darted some wild and hideous figure. Throwing itself upon the grass, it ran across the garden and into the darkness.

"Holmes," I whispered. "Did you see it? What was that?"

For the moment, Holmes was as startled as I. Then he broke into a low laugh.

"This is a strange household," he murmured. "That was the baboon."

I had forgotten the strange pets which the doctor kept. There was a cheetah, too, I remembered. And I hoped we might not find it leaping onto our shoulders. I confess that I felt easier when we climbed through the window and entered the bedroom.

Holmes quietly closed the shutters of the window. He moved the lamp to the table, and looked around the room. Everything was just the way we had seen it in the daytime. Holmes whispered very softly to me, "We must sit here without light. He would see it through the ventilator."

I nodded to show that I had heard.

"Do not fall asleep. Your life may depend on it. Have your pistol ready in case we should need it. I will sit on the side of the bed while you sit in that chair."

I took out my revolver and placed it on the corner of the table. Holmes had brought a long, thin cane with him. He placed it on the bed beside him. Near it he put a box of matches and the stump of a candle. Then he turned off the lamp.

I shall never forget those hours. The shutters completely cut off the light, and we waited in complete darkness. From outside, now and then, came the cry of a bird. And once, we heard a long cat-like yowl. This told us that the cheetah was wandering about. Far away we could hear the church clock striking the hours. Twelve struck, and one, and two, and three o'clock—and still we sat and waited silently for whatever might happen.

Suddenly, there was a brief gleam of light from the direction of the ventilator. It went out immediately. This was followed by a strong smell of burning oil and heated metal. Someone in the next room had lit a lantern. There was the soft sound of someone moving. Then all was silent once more.

For half an hour I sat listening carefully. Then suddenly I heard another sound—like that of a small jet of steam escaping from a kettle. The instant we heard it, Holmes jumped from the bed. He lit a match, grabbed his cane, and struck furiously at the bellpull.

"Do you see it, Watson!" he yelled. "Do you see it!"

But I saw nothing. I had heard a low, clear whistle. But I could not tell what it was at which my friend struck so furiously. I could, however, see that Holmes's face was deadly pale and was filled with horror and disgust.

Holmes had stopped lashing with his cane and was looking up at the ventilator. Suddenly, the silence of the night was broken by a horrible scream. It was a hoarse yell filled with anger, pain, and fear. They say that down in the village, that cry woke the sleepers in their beds. It struck cold to our hearts, and I stood gazing at Holmes until the last echoes of the cry had died away.

"What can that mean?" I gasped.

"It means that it is all over," Holmes answered. "Take your pistol, Watson, and we will enter Dr. Roylott's room."

With a grave face, Holmes lit the lamp and led the way down the hall. He knocked twice on the chamber door, but received no reply. Then he turned the handle and entered. I followed at his heels, pistol in hand.

It was a strange sight which met our eyes. On the table stood a lantern. It threw a brilliant beam of light on the iron safe whose door was thrown open. Beside the table, on the wooden chair, sat Dr. Grimesby Roylott. Across his lap lay the dog leash which we had noticed earlier that day.

Dr. Roylott's chin was pointed upward. His unmoving eyes were staring at the corner of the ceiling. Twisted around his forehead was a yellow band with brownish speckles.

"The band! The speckled band!" whispered Holmes.

I took a step forward. At that moment, the strange headband around the doctor's head began to move. There rose the diamond-shaped head and puffy neck of a snake.

"It's a swamp adder!" cried Holmes. "The deadliest snake in India. Dr. Roylott has died within ten seconds of being bitten! Quickly! Let us get this creature back into its den. Then we can alert Miss Stoner, and let the police know what has happened."

As he spoke, Holmes took the dog leash from the dead man's lap. Holmes slipped the noose around the snake's neck. Then, carrying it at arm's length, he thrust it into the safe and slammed shut the door.

———————◆———————

Such are the facts of the death of Dr. Grimesby Roylott of Stoke Moran. What I had not yet learned about the case was told to me by Holmes as we traveled home.

"It became clear," said Holmes to me in the cab, "that no one could enter the room from the window or the door. The floor and walls were solid, too. My attention was quickly drawn to the ventilator, and to the bell rope which hung down to the bed. I soon discovered that this was a dummy—and that the bed was nailed to the floor. This led me to suspect that the rope was there to provide a bridge—for something coming out of the ventilator hole and going down to the bed. The idea that it might be a snake came to me at once. And when I realized that the doctor had been obtaining animals from India, I felt sure I was on the right track."

Holmes shook his head sadly. "Dr. Roylott was both clever and cruel. He used the knowledge he had gained in India. He knew that the swamp adder's poison takes effect at once, and that it is one which cannot be discovered by any chemical test. Moreover, it was quite unlikely that anyone would notice the two tiny dark holes where the snake's fangs had struck.

"You will remember, of course, the whistling sound of which both sisters spoke. It was necessary for Dr. Roylott to call back the snake before it could be discovered in the morning light. Dr. Roylott had trained it, probably by using milk, to return to him when he whistled. He would put the snake through the ventilator late at night. He knew that it would crawl down the rope and land on the bed. It might or might not bite whoever was sleeping there. She might escape every night for a week. But sooner or later, she would become the snake's victim.

"I had come to these conclusions before I ever entered Dr. Roylott's room. A careful inspection of this chair showed me that he often stood on it. This was necessary, of course, to reach the ventilator. When I saw the safe, the saucer of milk, and the dog leash with the loop, I was certain I was right. The metallic clang heard by Miss Stoner was the safe closing to keep the snake in.

"Having once made up my mind, I took steps to obtain proof. Together we waited silently in the dark. Finally, when we heard the snake hiss, I quickly lit a match and attacked it with a cane."

"With the result that you drove it back through the ventilator."

"Where it turned upon its master. Angered by my blows, it struck at the first person it saw."

Holmes paused for a moment. "I fear," said he, "that I am indirectly responsible for the death of Dr. Roylott."

"Consider the nature of the man," said I. "And do not let it weigh too heavily upon your conscience."

At that moment, the cab stopped in front of our rooms on Baker Street. "And so, my dear Watson," said Holmes, "thus ends the mysterious Adventure of the Speckled Band."

Be a Reading Detective

Read each of the following questions. Then write the letter of the correct answer to each question. Remember, the symbol next to each question identifies the *kind* of reading skill that particular question helps you to develop.

1. Holmes was afraid that Watson would
   a. be in danger.
   b. help him very little.
   c. solve the case.
   d. lose interest quickly.

2. Why was the bed nailed to the floor?
   a. because it looked good there
   b. to make it easy to clean the room
   c. to keep it close to the ventilator
   d. so that it would not shake

3. Holmes and Watson saw a hideous figure dash wildly across the garden. What is the meaning of the word *hideous*?
   a. tiny
   b. slow
   c. ugly
   d. bulky

4. What did Holmes bring with him?
   a. a cane
   b. a pistol
   c. a rope
   d. a lantern

5. Which happened last?
   a. Holmes and Watson waited at the inn.
   b. The snake bit Dr. Roylott.
   c. Watson heard a low, clear whistle.
   d. Holmes extinguished the lantern.

6. " 'The band! The speckled band!' whispered Holmes." What was Holmes speaking about?
   a. a band of vagabonds
   b. something worn around the head
   c. a snake
   d. the dog leash

7. Which sentence expresses an opinion?
   a. " 'I fear,' said Holmes, 'that I am indirectly responsible for the death of Dr. Roylott.' "
   b. "Holmes quietly closed the shutters of the window."
   c. "Then suddenly, at the stroke of eleven, a single bright light shone out from the house."
   d. "Everything was just the way we had seen it in the daytime."

8. "With a grave face, Holmes lit the lamp and led the way down the hall." As used in this sentence, which word or expression means the same as *grave*?
   a. serious
   b. smiling
   c. hole in the ground
   d. mound of fresh earth

9. What is true of the swamp adder's poison?
   a. It is not very deadly.
   b. It takes effect after several hours.
   c. It takes effect at once.
   d. It paralyzes its victim.

10. Which sentence BEST tells what the story is mainly about?
   a. Two heads (Holmes and Dr. Watson) are better than one.
   b. Wild animals should not be kept as pets.
   c. The punishment fits the crime.
   d. It is dangerous to be left money.

Follow the Trail

Conclusions

A good reader makes or draws conclusions. **Conclusions** are decisions you come to about things in a story, based on facts and clues you read in that story. As the reader as detective, you must learn to draw conclusions. The following questions will help you practice this skill.

11. Julia Stoner was killed by

    a. her sister.

    b. a cougar or a cheetah.

    c. a snake.

    d. a servant.

12. Why was the ventilator added to the room?

    a. to give the house a modern look

    b. to give the room fresh air

    c. to let the swamp adder pass through

    d. to provide a servant's bellpull

13. The bell rope served as a kind of

    a. ladder.

    b. signal.

    c. whistle.

    d. decoration.

14. You can conclude that snakes

    a. come from India.

    b. are very small.

    c. like milk.

    d. cannot be trained.

15. Dr. Roylott planned Helen's death because

    a. she was soon to inherit her mother's money.

    b. she had told her story to Sherlock Holmes.

    c. he had always hated her.

    d. he did not want to take care of her.

Review the answers to the questions on page 36. How many of these conclusions had you already reached while you were reading the story? Share and discuss these conclusions with your classmates.

Find Word Meanings

The five words listed below appear in Part 3 of "The Adventure of the Speckled Band." Study the words and their definitions. Use the page numbers to check how the words are used in the story. Then complete the following sentences by using each vocabulary word only *once*.

word	meaning	page
assistance	help	28
prevent	stop; keep from happening	29
provide	offer; supply	32
obtaining	getting	32
inspection	the act of looking at closely	33

Sherlock Holmes undertook a careful _____16_____ of the rooms at Stoke Moran. He was interested in just one thing—_____17_____ clues. Holmes knew that clues would _____18_____ the answer to what had happened to Julia Stoner. Clues would lend _____19_____ to Holmes in his task. Holmes wanted to solve the case quickly, so he could _____20_____ the murderer from claiming another victim.

Look at Language

Noun-Adjective Pairs

Now that you've learned about nouns and adjectives, you can think about how they work together in stories to provide information and to powerfully describe people, places, events, and ideas.

Answer the following questions about nouns and adjectives in Part 3 of "The Adventure of the Speckled Band."

21. Identify the noun and adjective pair in the following sentence:

"At that moment, the lights in the old house at Stoke Moran went out and all was dark."

a. the lights
b. old house
c. went out
d. was dark

22. Which noun does the adjective *wild* describe in the following sentence:

"Suddenly, from out of a clump of bushes, there darted some wild and hideous figure."

a. clump
b. bushes
c. hideous
d. figure

23. Which noun and adjective pair could be used to replace "strange pets" in the following sentence:

"I had forgotten the strange pets which the doctor kept."

a. odd animals
b. weird patients
c. gentle creatures
d. crazy experiments

24. Read the following sentence from the story:

"Suddenly, the silence of the night was broken by a horrible scream."

Here, the author uses the adjective *horrible* to describe the *scream* so that

a. we can imagine what a terrible death Dr. Roylott died.
b. we can actually hear the scream, as the villagers did.
c. it will make sense that people were awakened by the scream.
d. Holmes will know it's safe to go into the next room.

25. Which is the most important adjective/noun pair in the story?

a. dog leash
b. bell rope
c. speckled band
d. whistling sound

Review the Case

The following activities will help you review and reflect on what happened in "The Adventure of the Speckled Band," Part 3.

1. Discuss. Which parts of the mystery did you figure out on your own, before reading the ending? Were you surprised by the solution to the clues?

2. Write. In a sentence or two explain how each of the following clues listed on pages 29–30 plays an important part in "The Adventure of the Speckled Band."

A. The dummy bell rope
B. The ventilator
C. The bed nailed to the floor
D. The whistling sound
E. The clanging sound
F. Julia Stoner's dying words
G. The saucer of milk
H. The safe
I. The dog leash
J. Dr. Roylott's love of animals from India

3. Technology Application. Look further into poisonous snakes of India. Try to find some pictures online of the kind of snake described in the story. Does such a snake, or one similar to it, actually exist? Explain your answer in a few sentences and include pictures, if possible.

**"It's all right, officer," he said. "I'm just
waiting for a friend. It's a date we
made twenty years ago."**

After Twenty Years

by O. Henry

The policeman on the beat moved up the avenue slowly. The time was nearly ten o'clock at night, but the streets were almost empty. Cold winds, with a threat of rain in them, had driven most people inside.

Trying doors as he went and twirling his club, he cast a watchful eye about. Now and then you might see the lights of an all-night luncheonette. But most of the doors belonged to business places that had been closed for many hours.

In the middle of a certain block, the policeman suddenly slowed his walk. In the doorway of a darkened hardware store stood a man with an unlighted cigar in his mouth. As the policeman walked up to him, the man spoke up quickly.

"It's all right, officer," he said. "I'm just waiting for a friend. It's a date we made twenty years ago."

The policeman stared at the man.

"Sounds a little funny to you, doesn't it?" said the man. "Well, I'll explain if you'd like to make certain it's on the level. About that long ago there used to be a restaurant where this store stands—'Big Joe' Brady's restaurant."

"Until five years ago," said the policeman. "It was torn down then."

The man in the doorway struck a match and lit his cigar. The light showed a pale, square-jawed face with sharp eyes and a vivid little white scar near his right eyebrow. The ends of his scarf were held together with a pin. In its center was a large diamond.

"Twenty years ago tonight," said the man, "I ate here at 'Big Joe' Brady's with Jimmy Wells, my best friend, and the greatest pal in the world. He and I were raised here in New York, just like two brothers. I was eighteen and Jimmy was twenty. The next morning I was to leave for the West to make my fortune. But you couldn't have dragged Jimmy out of New York. He thought it was the only place on earth. Well, we agreed that night that we would meet here again exactly twenty years from that date and time. We said we'd come—no matter how we were, or how far we had to travel. We figured that in twenty years each of us ought to have his future worked out and his reputation made, whatever they were going to be."

"It sounds pretty interesting," said the policeman. "Rather a long time between get-togethers, though, it seems to me. Haven't you heard from your friend since you left?"

"Well, yes, for a time we wrote," said the other. "But after a year or two we lost track of each other. You see, the West is a pretty big place, and I kept hopping around over it pretty lively. But I know Jimmy will meet me here if he's alive, for he always was the truest, most reliable old chap in the world. He'll never forget. I came a thousand miles to stand in this door tonight, and it's worth it if my old partner shows up."

The waiting man pulled out a handsome watch. Its hands were set with small diamonds.

"Three minutes to ten," he announced. "It was exactly ten o'clock when we parted here at the restaurant door."

"Did pretty well out West, didn't you?" asked the policeman.

"You bet! I hope Jimmy has done half as well. He was kind of a plodder, though, good fellow as he was. I've had to compete with some of the sharpest guys around to make my success. A man gets in a groove in New York. It takes the West to make him razor sharp."

The policeman twirled his club and took a step or two. "I'll be on my way. Hope your friend turns up all right. Going to call time on him sharp?"

"I should say not!" said the other. "I'll give him another half an hour at least. If Jimmy is alive on earth, he'll be here by that time. So long, officer."

"Good night," said the policeman, passing on along his beat, trying doors as he went.

There was now a light, cold rain falling, and the wind was blowing harder. The few people on the streets hurried quickly and silently along, their coat collars turned high, their hands in their pockets. And in the door of the hardware store stood the man who had come a thousand miles to keep a date with the friend of his youth. He smoked his cigar and waited.

About twenty minutes he waited. Then a tall man in a long overcoat with the collar turned up to his ears hurried across from the other side of the street. He went straight to the waiting man.

"Is that you, Bob?" he asked, uncertainly.

"Is that you, Jimmy Wells?" cried the man in the door.

"Bless my heart!" exclaimed the man who had just arrived. He grabbed the other man's hands with his own. "It's Bob, sure as fate. I was sure I'd find you here if you were still alive. Well, well, well!—twenty years is a long time. The old restaurant's gone, Bob. I wish it had lasted, so we could have another dinner there. How has the West treated you, old man?"

"Great. It has granted me everything I asked it for. Say, you've changed lots, Jimmy. You're two or three inches taller than I remembered."

"Oh, I grew a few inches after I was twenty."

"Doing well in New York, Jimmy?"

"Pretty well. I have a position in one of the city's departments. Come on, Bob. We'll go to a place I know of, and have a good long talk about old times."

The two men started up the street, arm in arm. The man from the West, pleased with his success, was talking about himself. The other, huddled in his overcoat, listened with interest.

At the corner stood a drugstore, bright with lights. When they came into this glare, each of them turned at the same moment to gaze upon the other's face.

The man from the West stopped suddenly and let go of the other man's arm.

"You're not Jimmy Wells!" he snapped. "Twenty years is a long time—but not long enough to change the shape of a man's nose."

"It sometimes changes a good man into a bad one," said the tall man. "You've been under arrest for ten minutes, 'Silky' Bob. We got word from Chicago that you were heading our way. They want to have a little talk with you. Going quietly, are you? That makes sense. Now before we go to the station, here's a note I was asked to hand to you. You may read it here at the window. It's from Patrolman Wells."

The man from the West unfolded the little piece of paper that was handed to him. His hand was steady when he began to read it. But it trembled a little by the time he had finished. The note was rather short.

Now it's time for YOU to be the Reader as Detective.

What do you think Patrolman Wells's note said? Read on to see if you are right!

Bob: I was at the meeting place on time. When you struck the match to light your cigar, I saw it was the face of the man wanted in Chicago. Somehow I couldn't do it myself, so I went and got a plainclothes man to do the job.

Jimmy

Be a Reading Detective

Read each of the following questions. Then write the letter of the correct answer to each question. Remember, the symbol next to each question identifies the *kind* of reading skill that particular question helps you to develop.

1. Which BEST expresses the main idea of the story?
   a. People never change.
   b. A policeman places loyalty to duty over loyalty to friendship.
   c. One should never trust old friends.
   d. Over enough time, people can become unrecognizable.

2. The man in the doorway, Bob, had everything except
   a. a square jaw
   b. a tan face
   c. a scar near his eyebrow
   d. a cigar in his mouth

3. "Silky" Bob was wearing
   a. a long overcoat with the collar turned up.
   b. expensive jewelry.
   c. an old jacket.
   d. a silk shirt

4. You can infer that Jimmy Wells
   a. was unhappy about being a policeman.
   b. hated "Silky" Bob.
   c. was sorry to have his friend arrested.
   d. failed to become a success.

5. Bob thought that Jimmy was "the truest, most reliable old chap in the world." Which word or expression BEST defines the word *reliable*?
   a. wealthy
   b. worthy of trust
   c. long forgotten
   d. lazy

6. What happened last in the story?
   a. The plainclothes man gave "Silky" Bob a letter.
   b. The policeman twirled his club and went on his way.
   c. Bob left for the West to make his fortune.
   d. Jimmy came to meet his old friend.

7. You can infer that Jimmy asked Bob how long he would wait for his friend because Jimmy
   a. was getting cold.
   b. wasn't sure the man was "Silky" Bob.
   c. wanted to make certain that Bob would wait there.
   d. didn't believe he was who he said he was.

8. Which BEST describes the evening?

   a. bright and clear
   b. warm and pleasant
   c. cold and dark
   d. cool and crisp

9. "At the corner stood a drugstore, bright with lights. When they came into this glare, each of them turned at the same moment to gaze upon the other's face." As used in this sentence, the word *glare* means

   a. stare.
   b. light.
   c. anger.
   d. stick out.

10. Which of the following is an opinion?

    a. Bob and Jimmy were once the best of friends.
    b. Jimmy arrived at the meeting place on time.
    c. "Silky" Bob was probably angry at Jimmy for turning him in.
    d. Bob and Jimmy had set the date to meet twenty years earlier.

Follow the Trail

Story Clues

O. Henry, the author of "After Twenty Years," is famous for his surprise endings. However, his stories usually contain *clues* that suggest how the story will end. A careful reader can learn to detect, or spot, these clues and use them to guess how the story will end.

How good a reading detective are you? Did you spot some clues to the "surprise" ending in the story? Answer the questions on the next page. They will give you practice in discovering clues in a story.

11. The man in the overcoat told Bob, "Oh, I grew a few inches after I was twenty." This is a clue that the man was not Jimmy Wells because

a. Jimmy Wells was still out west.
b. the man in the overcoat was taller than Jimmy.
c. it is unusual for someone to grow a few inches after the age of twenty.
d. Jimmy Wells had always been very tall.

12. The man in the overcoat told Bob, "I have a position in one of the city's departments." This was true. For what department did he work?

a. the police department
b. the housing department
c. the department of transportation
d. the electric department

13. The new arrival stayed "huddled in his overcoat" with the "collar turned up to his ears." Why?

a. He thought he looked good that way.
b. He didn't want "Silky" Bob to see his face.
c. He was wearing someone else's coat.
d. He was very cold late at night.

14. Although it was very dark, the man in the overcoat "hurried across from the other side of the street" and "went straight to the waiting man." This suggests that the man in the overcoat

a. wasn't sure who the other man was.
b. already knew who the other man was.
c. didn't want to meet his old friend.
d. needed help from the other man.

15. The author describes the waiting man as "razor sharp" with a "white scar near his right eyebrow." He also has a large diamond scarf pin and a handsome watch set with diamonds. Possibly, this is O. Henry's way of suggesting that the man

a. has become wealthy in ways that are not honest.
b. is not as rich as he appears to be.
c. is quiet and shy although he is wealthy.
d. wears fake jewelry to impress people.

Find Word Meanings

The five words listed below appear in "After Twenty Years." Study the words and their definitions. Use the page numbers to check how the words are used in the story. Then complete the following sentences by using each vocabulary word only *once*.

word	meaning	page
vivid	lively; clear; distinct	42
reputation	good name; fame	42
compete	try to win something wanted by others	42
granted	given; awarded	43
steady	changing little; firm	44

O. Henry is one of America's best-known short story writers. He gained his _____16_____ , or fame, through the use of the "unexpected" or "surprise" ending. This gives his work a special style. He is also known for creating characters who are lively, _____17_____ , and distinct.

From 1900 to 1910, O. Henry wrote a _____18_____ stream of short stories. He wrote about 600 in all. O. Henry loved New York City, so he used it as the setting for many of these stories.

Today, writers _____19_____ for a prize called the O. Henry Award. It is _____20_____ to the person who writes the best American short story each year.

Look at Language

Context Clues

Often, you can figure out the meaning of a difficult or unfamiliar word by looking at the *context*—the words (and sometimes the sentences) around the word. **Context clues** will help you find the word's meaning.

As the Reader as Detective, you have already had experience using vocabulary clues to figure out word meanings. The following questions will provide additional practice in using context clues to find the word's meaning.

21. In the first sentence, the word *beat* might be replaced by

    a. street.
    b. patrol.
    c. rhythm.
    d. store.

22. What might a "luncheonette" be, as mentioned in the second paragraph?

    a. a streetlight
    b. a store
    c. a restaurant
    d. a hiding place

23. What does Bob mean when he says he was going west to make his "fortune"?

    a. He was going to become famous.
    b. He was going to become a criminal.
    c. He was going to leave his friend.
    d. He was going to make money.

24. What did Bob most likely mean when he said Jimmy was "kind of a plodder"?

    a. Jimmy was always an honest man.
    b. Jimmy "plodded along," not really trying to be great.
    c. Jimmy followed what everyone else did.
    d. Jimmy was not a very smart man.

25. The second man who approaches Bob is "huddled in this overcoat." Another word for *huddled* in that context might be

    a. quiet.
    b. hunched.
    c. protected.
    d. walking.

Review the Case

The following activities will help you review and reflect on what happened in "After Twenty Years."

1. **Discuss.** What do you think of Jimmy Wells's decision to turn in his friend? Might you have done the same thing if you were in his position? Explain.

2. **Write.** "After Twenty Years" ends with a note from Jimmy to Bob. Suppose Bob could answer Jimmy's note. What do you think he would say? Write a brief note from Bob to Jimmy. Try not to have Bob express anger in his answer. First make a rough copy of the note. Then proofread and correct it. Afterward, write your final copy.

3. **Technology Application.** Go online to find a free podcast of "After Twenty Years" or another O. Henry story. What did you get out of listening to the story that you didn't get from reading it, and vice versa? Write a brief reflection describing your experience. If you can't obtain a podcast, read it aloud in class by having different people play each character and someone read the narration. Then reflect on the experience.

Sarah Tops

by Isaac Asimov

I came out of the Museum of Natural History and was crossing the street on my way to the subway. That's when I saw the crowd about halfway down the block. I saw the police cars, too. I could hear the whine of an ambulance.

For a minute I hesitated. But then I walked on. Folks who are curious just get in the way of people trying to save lives. Dad, who's a detective on the force, complains about that all the time.

I just kept my mind on the term paper I was going to have to write on air pollution for my 8th-grade class. I thought about the notes I had taken on the subject while I was at the museum.

Of course, I knew I would read about what had happened in the museum in tomorrow's newspaper. Besides, I would ask Dad about it after dinner. He sometimes talked about cases without telling too much of the real private details.

After Dad told us, Mom looked kind of worried. She said, "The man was killed in the museum. You were in the museum, Larry."

I said, "I was working on my term paper. I got there early in the morning."

Mom looked very worried. "There might have been shooting in the museum."

"Well, there wasn't," said Dad, softly. "This man tried to hide himself there and he didn't succeed."

"I would have," I said. "I know the museum, every inch."

Dad doesn't like me bragging. So he frowned a little and said, "They didn't let him get away entirely. They caught up with him outside. They knifed him and got away. We'll catch them, though. We know who they are."

He nodded his head. "They're what's left of that gang that broke into that jewelry store two weeks ago. We managed to get the jewels back. But we didn't grab all the men. We didn't get all the jewels back either. One diamond was left. A big one—worth $30,000."

"Maybe that's what the killers were after," I said.

"Very likely. The dead man was probably trying to cross up the other two. He was probably trying to get away with that one stone for himself. They turned out his pockets, nearly ripped off his clothes, after they knifed him."

"Did they get the diamond?" I asked.

"How can we tell? The woman who reported the killing found him when he was just barely alive. She said he said three words to her, very slowly, 'Try—Sarah—Tops.' Then he died."

"Who is Sarah Tops?" asked Mom.

Dad shrugged. "I don't know. I don't even know if that's really what he said. The woman was pretty hysterical. If she's right and that's what he said, then maybe the killers didn't get the diamond. Maybe the dead man left it with Sarah Tops, whoever she is."

"Is there a Sarah Tops in the phone book, Dad?" I asked.

Dad said, "Did you think we didn't look? No Sarah Tops, either with one *P* or two *P*s. Nothing in the city phone book. Nothing in our files. Nothing in the FBI files."

Mom said, "Maybe it's not a person. Maybe it's a company. Sarah Tops cakes or something."

"Could be," said Dad. "There's no Sarah Tops company. But there are other kinds of Tops companies. They'll be checked for anyone working there named Sarah."

Suddenly I got an idea and bubbled over. "Listen, Dad, maybe it isn't a company either. Maybe it's a *thing*. Maybe the woman didn't hear 'Sarah Tops' but heard 'Sarah's top.' You know, a *top* that you *spin*. If the dead guy has a daughter named Sarah, maybe he cut a bit out of her top and stashed the diamond inside. Maybe—"

Dad grinned. "Very good, Larry," he said. "But he doesn't have a daughter named Sarah. Or any relative by that name as far as we know. We've searched where he lived. There's nothing reported there that can be called a top."

I felt sort of let down and disappointed. "Well," I said, "I suppose that's not such a good idea anyway. Because why should he say we ought to *try* it? He either hid it in Sarah's top or he didn't. He would know which. Why should he say we should *try* it?"

And then it hit me. What if—

I said, "Dad, can you get into the museum this late?"

"On police business? Sure."

"Dad," I said, kind of breathless, "I think we better go look. *Now*. Before the people start coming in again."

"Why?"

"I've got a silly idea. I—I—"

Dad didn't push me. He likes me to have my own ideas. He thinks maybe I'll be a detective too, some day. He said, "All right. Let's follow up your lead."

We got there just when the last purple bit of twilight was turning to black. We were let in by a guard.

I'd never been in the museum when it was dark. It looked like a huge underground cave. The guard's flashlight made things even more mysterious.

We took the elevator up to the fourth floor. I could see the big shapes in the bit of light that shone this way and that as the guard moved his flashlight. "Do you want me to put on the light in this room?" he asked.

"Yes, please," I said.

There they all were. Some were in glass cases. But the big ones were in the middle of the large room. Bones and teeth and spines of giants that ruled the earth millions of years ago. I said, "I want to look close at that one. Is it all right if I climb over the railing?"

"Go ahead," said the guard. He helped me.

I leaned against the platform. I was looking at the gray plaster material that the dinosaur was standing on.

Suddenly I spotted something. "What's this?" I said. It didn't look much different in color from the plaster.

"Chewing gum," said the guard, frowning. "Those darn kids—"

I said, "The guy was trying to get away. He saw his chance to throw this—to hide it from the gang—"

Dad took the gum from me. He squeezed the gum. Then he pulled it apart. Inside, something caught the light and flashed. Dad put the diamond in an envelope. Then he said to me, "How did you know?"

Now it's time for YOU to be the Reader as Detective.

How did Larry know where to look for the diamond? Think back to what the dying man said. Then read on.

I said, "Just look at that."

It was an amazing dinosaur. It had a large skull with long bones stretching back over the neck. It had two horns over the eyes, and a third one, just a bump, on the nose. The nameplate said: Triceratops.

Be a Reading Detective

Read each of the following questions. Then write the letter of the correct answer to each question. Remember, the symbol next to each question identifies the *kind* of reading skill that particular question helps you to develop.

1. The man was killed
   a. in a jewelry store.
   b. on his way to the subway.
   c. in the Museum of Natural History.
   d. in the library.

2. Dad said that the diamond was worth

    a. $300.
    b. $3,000.
    c. $30,000.
    d. $300,000.

3. What happened after the guard turned on the light in the museum?

    a. Larry began to look through the notes he had taken.
    b. Larry climbed over the railing.
    c. They all took the elevator to the fourth floor.
    d. They all searched around the dinosaur.

4. Larry's father was "a detective on the force." As used in this sentence, what is the meaning of the word *force*?

    a. power
    b. police or military organization
    c. group of museum workers
    d. strength

5. Why do you think Larry wanted to return to the museum right away?

    a. He wanted to get there before the sun came out.
    b. He was afraid that someone else might find the diamond first.
    c. He thought that the murderer might be hiding there.
    d. He was excited about the idea he had.

6. Larry's dad thought that Larry might become a

    a. scientist.
    b. detective.
    c. teacher.
    d. security guard.

7. Which is *not* an opinion?

   a. The Museum of Natural History is the best museum in the world.
   b. Isaac Asimov is the author of "Sarah Tops."
   c. Being a detective is the most dangerous job anyone can have.
   d. Kids are good at solving complex mysteries.

8. When Larry's dad says "Let's follow up your lead," he means that they will

   a. follow Larry to the museum, since he knows how to get there.
   b. check into Larry's idea to see if he's right.
   c. let Larry take over the case.
   d. follow the person Larry suspects.

9. Larry said that he knew

   a. every inch of the museum.
   b. how to get into the museum.
   c. the name of the murderer.
   d. where the diamond was.

10. Suppose this story appeared as a news article in a newspaper. Which of the following would make the BEST headline?

   a. Detective's Son Solves Museum Murder Case
   b. Man Tries to Hide in Museum—Doesn't Succeed
   c. Larry and His Father Discuss Man Killed in Museum
   d. Sarah Tops Found Guilty in Robbery

Follow the Trail

Conclusions

As you've learned, a good reader makes or draws conclusions. **Conclusions** are decisions you come to about things in a story, based on facts and clues you read in that story. As the Reader as Detective, you must learn to draw conclusions. The following questions will help you practice this skill.

11. You can conclude that the dying man
- a. gave the diamond to Sarah Tops.
- b. nearly got away from his killers.
- c. hid the diamond in the chewing gum.
- d. wasn't a very good thief.

12. The prefix *tri-* means *three*. Therefore, the dinosaur was probably called *triceratops* because it had
- a. three horns.
- b. three toes on each foot.
- c. three sharp fangs in the front of its mouth.
- d. three spikes on its back.

13. It was hard to find the gum because
- a. the room was so dark.
- b. it was almost the same color as the plaster.
- c. it wasn't hidden in the museum.
- d. it had dried on the platform.

14. Larry's actions suggest that he is
- a. thoughtful and smart.
- b. a poor student.
- c. smart but lazy.
- d. too energetic.

15. It is correct to conclude that
- a. some kids stuck the gum on the plaster.
- b. the guard knew where the diamond was hidden.
- c. the dying man was trying to say "triceratops."
- d. Sarah Tops was related to the thief.

Find Word Meanings

The five words listed below appear in "Sarah Tops." Study the words and their definitions. Use the page numbers to check how the words are used in the story. Then complete the following sentences by using each vocabulary word only *once*.

word	meaning	page
pollution	dirt and poison that affect the growth of life	51
bragging	praising or boasting about oneself	52
entirely	completely	52
hysterical	highly excited; out of control	52
stashed	hid	52

Jordan could not find the report he had written for science class on air _____16_____ . After searching for it for half an hour, he was so upset that he was nearly _____17_____ . He had spent a long time working on the paper, and now it was missing. To make matters worse, he had even been _____18_____ to his friends about how good it was. If he could not find it, he was going to be embarrassed in class.

Jordan began to search the room again. He had already looked through it _____19_____ . Suddenly, Jordan remembered something. For safekeeping, he had _____20_____ the report in the bottom drawer of his desk. Jordan let out a huge sigh of relief when he saw the report lying safely there.

Look at Language

Synonyms

Synonyms are words that have the same or nearly the same meanings. For example, the words *throw* and *toss* are synonyms. The words *large*, *enormous*, and *huge* are synonyms, too. Authors use synonyms to make their writing more interesting. And by using synonyms, it is possible to obtain a precise, or exact, shade of meaning.

The following questions ask about synonyms of words in "Sarah Tops."

21. "Folks who are curious just get in the way of people trying to save lives."

Another word for *folks* is

a. people.
b. parents.
c. cops.
d. kids.

22. "For a minute I hesitated. But then I walked on."

A synonym for *hesitated* is

a. panicked.
b. paused.
c. hurried.
d. stopped.

23. "Suddenly I spotted something. 'What's this?' I said."

Another word for *spotted* is

a. searched.
b. noticed.
c. stained.
d. grabbed.

24. "Dad grinned. 'Very good, Larry,' he said."

A synonym for *grinned* is

a. frowned.
b. stared.
c. smiled.
d. brightened.

25. "Because why should he say we ought to *try* it?"

A synonym for *ought* is

a. should.
b. forgot.
c. could.
d. shouldn't.

Review the Case

The following activities will help you review and reflect on what happened in "Sarah Tops."

1. Discuss. If you had something important or valuable to hide, how might you go about making sure it stayed safe? Choose something you'd feel comfortable discussing with your classmates.

2. Write. Larry's dad must have been proud of Larry for having solved the case. What do you think he might have told the other detectives at the station house later? In a paragraph, write what you think Larry's father might have said. Be sure to put quotation marks around his words.

Afterward, share your writing with the class and select the compositions you liked best.

3. Technology Application. Look at the Web site for a natural history museum close to you. Find at least one article or exhibit that interests you. Write a paragraph or two about what you find.

**The girl was staring out through the
open window. There was a look of
dazed horror in her eyes.**

The Open Window

by Saki

"**M**y aunt will be down in a few minutes, Mr. Nuttel,"
said a very calm young lady of fifteen. "But for now, you must try
to put up with me."

Framton Nuttel looked at the young lady. He tried to think of
something polite to say to her. But he was very nervous. In fact, he
had come to the country as a cure for his nerves. And talking to
strangers only got him more upset.

"I know how it will be," Framton's sister had said, when he
was getting ready to leave. "You will stay by yourself down there
in the country. You won't say a word to a living soul. Then your
nerves will be worse than ever. Look, I'll give you the names of
people I met there. Some of them, I remember, seemed quite nice."

Framton wondered if Mrs. Sappleton was one of the "nice"
ones.

Several moments of silence passed. Then the young lady's voice
broke the silence. "Do you know many people around here?" she
asked.

"Hardly a soul," said Framton. "My sister lived in this area
four years ago. She gave me a letter of introduction to Mrs.
Sappleton."

"Then you know almost nothing about my aunt?" asked the
calm young lady.

"Only her name and address," admitted Framton.

He was wondering if Mrs. Sappleton was married. Something about the room seemed to suggest that a man lived there.

"Her great tragedy happened just three years ago," said the girl. "That was after your sister left."

"Her tragedy?" asked Framton. Somehow in this restful country spot tragedies seemed out of place.

"You may wonder why we keep that window wide open on an October afternoon," said the niece. She pointed to a large French window that opened onto the lawn.

"It is quite warm for this time of year," said Framton. "But has that window got anything to do with the tragedy?"

"Out through that window, exactly three years ago today, her husband and her two brothers went off hunting. They never came back. They were drowned, all three. It had been that terribly wet summer, you know. Places that were safe in other years gave way suddenly without warning. Their bodies were never found. That was the worst part of it."

Here, for the first time, the girl's voice became less calm. It began to crack. "Poor dear aunt always thinks that they will come back some day. They and the little brown dog that was lost with them. She believes that they will walk through that window, just as they used to. That is why the window is always kept open until dark."

The girl paused and shook her head sadly. "Poor dear aunt. She has often told me how they went out. Her husband had his raincoat over his arm. Ronnie, her younger brother, was singing 'It's a long way to Tipperary.' He always did that to tease her. She said it got on her nerves. Do you know, sometimes, on still, quiet evenings like this, I almost get a creepy feeling that they will all walk in through that window. . . ."

She broke off with a little shudder. It was a relief to Framton when the aunt burst into the room. She apologized for being so late.

"I hope Vera has been amusing you," she said.

"She has been very . . . interesting," said Framton.

"I hope you don't mind the open window," said Mrs. Sappleton brightly. "My husband and brothers will be home soon from hunting. They always come in that way. They've been out in the marsh, so they'll certainly mess up my poor carpets. So like you menfolk, isn't it?"

She chatted cheerfully about hunting. She went on about how few birds there were that season, and how to find ducks in the winter. It was horrible to Framton. He tried again and again, without success, to change the subject. But Mrs. Sappleton was hardly listening to him. Her eyes kept looking past him to the open window and the lawn beyond. It certainly was unlucky that he should have come visiting just three years to the day when her family was lost.

"The doctors agree that I must have complete rest," said Framton. "I must not have any kind of excitement at all. On the matter of my diet, they are really not sure."

"No?" said Mrs. Sappleton, holding back a yawn. But suddenly she brightened into alert attention—but not at what Framton was saying.

"Here they are at last!" she cried. "Just in time for tea. And don't they look muddy up to their eyes!"

Framton shivered slightly and turned to give the girl a knowing look. But the girl was staring out through the open window. There was a look of dazed horror in her eyes. In a chill shock of nameless fear, Framton swung round in his seat. He looked in the same direction.

In the darkening twilight, three figures were walking across the lawn towards the window. They all carried guns under their arms. One of them had a raincoat thrown over his shoulder. A tired brown dog kept close at their heels. Quietly they neared the house. Then a deep young voice sang out, "It's a long way to Tipperary!"

Framton jumped out of his chair. He wildly grabbed his hat. Within seconds he had raced down the hall, up the road, and through the front gate. A man riding a bicycle had to drive into the bushes to avoid an accident.

"Here we are, my dear," said the man with the raincoat. "It's a bit muddy out, but most of it's dry. Who was that who dashed out as we came up?"

"A very strange man, a Mr. Nuttel," said Mrs. Sappleton. "He could talk only about how ill he was, and bolted off without a word when you arrived. One would think he had seen a ghost."

Now it's time for YOU to be the Reader as Detective.

What do you think Vera answered? What do you think she might have said?

Read on to see if you are right!

"It probably was our dog," said Vera calmly. "He told me he had a terrible fear of dogs. Once, in India, he was chased into a cemetery by a pack of wild dogs. He had to spend the night in a newly dug grave, with the creatures barking and snarling just above him. That would make anyone nervous."

Vera loved to make up stories on the spot. She was really quite good at it.

Be a Reading Detective

Read each of the following questions. Then write the letter of the correct answer to each question. Remember, the symbol next to each question identifies the *kind* of reading skill that particular question helps you to develop.

1. Framton had come to the country to
   a. enjoy nature.
   b. visit his sister.
   c. cure his nerves.
   d. see old friends.

2. You can infer that Mrs. Sappleton's husband and brothers

  a. were drowned while hunting.
  b. were never lost at all.
  c. returned after several years.
  d. had a favorite hunting spot.

3. Framton's sister gave him

  a. a letter of introduction.
  b. a cup of tea.
  c. a house to live in.
  d. some strong medicine.

4. "Places that were safe in other years gave way suddenly without warning." If something *gave way*, it means that it

  a. exploded.
  b. sank.
  c. disappeared.
  d. led the way.

5. Which happened last?

  a. Mrs. Sappleton chatted cheerfully about hunting.
  b. Framton explained that he needed complete rest.
  c. Vera stared in horror through the open window.
  d. Framton's sister introduced him to people.

6. Which of the following is a fact?

  a. "Something in the room seemed to suggest that a man lived there."
  b. Mrs. Sappleton hardly listened to Framton.
  c. "It probably was our dog" that scared Framton, Vera said.
  d. "That [barking] would make anyone nervous."

7. At the end of the story, Framton probably thought that

a. he was seeing ghosts.

b. Vera had been lying to him.

c. Mrs. Sappleton was surprised to see her family.

d. the dog would attack him.

8. Mrs. Sappleton stated that Framton had "bolted off without a word." As used in this sentence, what is the meaning of the word *bolted*?

a. fastened

b. nailed

c. raced

d. changed

9. According to Vera, when had the "great tragedy" happened?

a. three years ago

b. four years ago

c. 15 years ago

d. one year ago

10. Which sentence BEST expresses the main idea of the story?

a. Three men return home from hunting.

b. A young storyteller strikes again.

c. Framton Nuttel has a terrible fear of dogs.

d. The countryside is a good cure for nerves.

Follow the Trail

Characters

To fully enjoy and appreciate what you are reading, you must recognize and understand the characters' different personalities and beliefs. In "The Open Window," for example, Framton's personality plays an important part in the story. The following questions will help you think about characters.

11. Which group of words BEST describes Framton Nuttel?
    a. witty and charming
    b. nervous and uncomfortable
    c. friendly and amusing
    d. angry and unpleasant

12. Which sentence BEST characterizes Vera?
    a. She was quite dull.
    b. She was very shy.
    c. She had a lively imagination.
    d. She was very funny.

13. Mrs. Sappleton thought that Framton was
    a. rather boring and strange.
    b. very interesting.
    c. a good match for Vera.
    d. an annoying man.

14. Which of the following is true of Vera?
    a. She was a very fine actress.
    b. She was afraid of strangers.
    c. She hated telling stories.
    d. She spent a lot of time alone.

15. When Framton saw the hunters, he found it especially shocking because
    a. he was easily excited.
    b. he needed quiet and rest.
    c. both of the above.
    d. none of the above.

Find Word Meanings

The five words listed below appear in "The Open Window." Study the words and their definitions. Use the page numbers to check how the words are used in the story. Then complete the following sentences by using each vocabulary word only *once*.

word	meaning	page
introduction	beginning or starting point; making known	61
tragedy	a terrible happening; unusual sadness	62
shudder	shake with fear	63
alert	wide-awake; very watchful	63
chill	make cold; sudden coldness	63

"The Open Window" is a good beginning, or _____16_____, to the tales of Saki. This story is typical of his work. It begins in a very simple manner. But its conclusion may make you either _____17_____ or laugh.

Some of Saki's stories are very amusing. Others, however, end on a note of _____18_____. The scarier stories can _____19_____ you to the bone.

Saki and O. Henry are similar in style. Both authors like to surprise their readers. Therefore, be especially _____20_____ when you read their works.

Look at Language

Antonyms

As you've learned, synonyms are words that have the same or nearly the same meanings. **Antonyms**, on the other hand, are words that have *opposite* meanings. Some examples of antonyms are *always* and *never*, *up* and *down*, *near* and *far*.

The following questions about "The Open Window" will give you practice in identifying antonyms.

21. Which two words from the first two paragraphs of the story are antonyms?

a. polite-nervous
b. think-cure
c. calm-nervous
d. country-upset

22. "Several moments of silence passed. Then the young lady's voice broke the silence. 'Do you know many people around here?' she asked."

" 'Hardly a soul,' said Framton."

Which is the BEST antonym for *hardly* as it is used above?

a. barely
b. completely
c. rarely
d. harshly

23. Which has the opposite meaning of *restful*?

a. peaceful
b. lively
c. confusing
d. beautiful

24. When Mrs. Sappleton enters the room, she says, "I hope Vera has been amusing you." Which is an antonym for *amusing* in this sentence?

a. boring
b. entertaining
c. deceiving
d. scaring

25. Below are four pairs of words from the story. Which pair are *not* antonyms?

a. sadly-brightly
b. rest-excitement
c. dry-wet
d. horror-fear

Review the Case

The following activities will help you review and reflect on what happened in "The Open Window."

1. Discuss. Vera asked, "Then you know almost nothing about my aunt?" "Only her name and address," admitted Framton. In a group discussion, explain why you think Vera asked this question and why the information she received was so important.

2. Write. Suppose Framton Nuttel wrote a letter to his sister telling about his visit to Mrs. Sappleton's home. What do you think he would say? Pretend you are Framton Nuttel. Write a letter to "Dear Sister," describing your visit. First make a rough draft of your letter. Make corrections. Then write your final draft. Later, you and your classmates can exchange letters. Which ones did you like best? Why?

3. Technology Application. "It's a Long Way to Tipperary" is a famous song, but you may have never heard it. Research its history on the Internet. Search for an audio version that you can listen to. Discuss why the author might have chosen this song for the story.

"Take over," I said. "Don't let this guy ruin your career." "I'll try it," the kid said...

One Throw

by W. C. Heinz

I checked into a hotel called the Olympia, which is right on the main street and the only hotel in the town. After lunch I was hanging around the lobby, and I got to talking to the guy at the desk. I asked him if this wasn't the town where that kid named Maneri played ball.

"That's right," the guy said. "He's a pretty good ballplayer."

"He should be," I said. "I read that he was the new Phil Rizzuto."*

"That's what they said," the guy said.

"What's the matter with him?" I said. "I mean—if he's such a good ballplayer, what's he doing in this league?"

"I don't know," the guy said. "I guess the Yankees know what they're doing."

"He lives here in this hotel?"

"That's right," the guy said. "Most of the older ballplayers stay in rooming houses, but Pete and a couple other kids live here.

He was leaning on the desk, talking to me and looking across the little lobby. He nodded his head. "Here he comes now."

The kid had come through the door from the street. I could see why, when he showed up with the Yankees in spring training, he made them all think of Rizzuto. He isn't any bigger than Rizzuto, and he looks just like him.

---

*Phil Rizzuto: a great baseball player for the New York Yankees. Rizzuto, who was five feet six inches tall, played shortstop.

"Hello, Nick," he said to the guy at the desk.

"Hello, Pete," the guy at the desk said. "How goes it today?"

"All right," the kid said, but you could see that he was exaggerating.

"I'm sorry, Pete," the guy at the desk said, "but no mail today."

"That's all right, Nick," the kid said. "I'm used to it."

"Excuse me," I said, "but you're Pete Maneri?"

"That's right," the kid said, turning and looking at me.

"Excuse me," the guy at the desk said, introducing us. "Pete, this is Mr. Franklin."

"Harry Franklin," I said.

"I'm glad to know you," the kid said, shaking my hand.

"I recognize you from your pictures," I said.

"Pete's a good ballplayer," the guy at the desk said.

"Not very," the kid said.

"Don't take his word for it, Mr. Franklin," the guy said.

"I'm a great ball fan," I said to the kid. "Do you people play tonight?"

"We play two games," the kid said.

"That first game's at six o'clock," the guy at the desk said. "They play pretty good ball."

"I'll be there," I said. "I used to play a little ball myself."

"You did?" the kid said.

"With Columbus," I said. "That was twenty years ago."

"Is that right?" the kid said . . .

That's the way I got to talking with the kid. They had one of those pine-paneled grill rooms in the basement of the hotel, and we went down there. I had a cup of coffee and the kid had a Coke, and I told him a few stories and he turned out to be a real good listener.

"But what do you do now, Mr. Franklin?" he said after a while.

"I sell hardware," I said. "I can think of some things I'd like better, but I was going to ask you how you like playing in this league."

"Well," the kid said, "I guess I've got no kick coming."

"Oh, I don't know," I said. "I understand you're too good for this league. What are they trying to do to you?"

"I don't know," the kid said. "I can't understand it."

"What's the trouble?"

"Well," the kid said, "there's nothing wrong with my playing. I'm hitting .365 right now. I lead the league in stolen bases. There's nobody can field with me, but who cares?"

"Who manages this ball club?"

"Al Dall," the kid said. "You remember, he played in the outfield for the Yankees for about four years."

"I remember."

"Maybe he's all right," the kid said, "but I don't get along with him. He's on my neck all the time."

"Well," I said, "that's the way they are in the minors sometimes. You have to remember the guy is looking out for himself and his ball club first."

"I know that," the kid said. "If I get the big hit or make the play, he never says anything. The other night I tried to take second on a loose ball and I got caught in the rundown. He bawled me out in front of everybody. There's nothing I can do."

"Oh, I don't know," I said. "This is probably a guy who knows he's got a good thing in you, and he's trying to keep you around. You people lead the league, and that makes him look good. He doesn't want to lose you to Kansas City or the Yankees."

"That's what I mean," the kid said. "When the Yankees sent me down here they said, 'Don't worry. We'll keep an eye on you.' So Dall never sends back a good report on me. Nobody ever comes down to look me over. What chance is there for a guy like Eddie Brown to see me in this town?"

"You have to remember that Eddie Brown's the big shot," I said, "the great Yankee scout."

"Sure," the kid said, "and I'll never see him in this place. I have an idea that if they ever ask Dall about me, he keeps knocking me down."

"Why don't you go after Dall?" I said. "I had trouble like that once myself, but I figured out a way to get attention."

"You did?" the kid said.

"I threw a couple of balls over the first baseman's head," I said. "I threw a couple of games away, and that really made the manager sore. So what does he do? He blows the whistle on me, and what happens? That gets the top brass curious, and they send down to see what's wrong."

"Is that so?" the kid said. "What happened?"

"Two weeks later," I said, "I was up with Columbus."

"Is that right?" the kid said.

"Sure," I said, egging him on. "What have you got to lose?"

"Nothing," the kid said. "I haven't got anything to lose."

"I'd try it," I said.

"I might," the kid said. "I might try it tonight if the spot comes up."

I could see from the way he said it that he was madder than he'd said. Maybe you think this is mean to steam a kid up like this, but I do some strange things.

"Take over," I said. "Don't let this guy ruin your career."

"I'll try it," the kid said. "Are you coming out to the park tonight?"

"I wouldn't miss it," I said. "This will be better than making out route sheets and sales orders."

It's not much of a ball park in this town—old wooden bleachers and an old wooden fence and about four hundred people in the stands. The first game wasn't much of a game either, with the home club winning something like 8 to 1.

The kid didn't have any hard chances, but I could see he was a ballplayer, with a double and a couple of walks and a lot of speed.

The second game was different, though. The other club got a couple of runs and then the home club picked up three runs in one inning. In the top of the ninth the home club had a 3–2 lead and two outs when the pitching began to fall apart and the other club loaded the bases.

I was trying to wish the ball down to the kid, just to see what he'd do with it, when the batter drove one on one bounce to the kid's right.

The kid was off for it when the ball started. He made a back-hand stab and grabbed it. He was deep now, and he turned in the air and fired. If it goes over the first baseman's head it's two runs in and a panic—but it's the prettiest throw you'd want to see. It's right on a line, and the runner is out by a step, and it's the ball game.

I walked back to the hotel, thinking about the kid. I sat around the lobby until I saw him come in, and then I walked toward the elevator as if I were going to my room, but so I'd meet him. I could see he didn't want to talk.

"How about a Coke?" I said.

"No," he said. "Thanks, but I'm going to bed."

"Look," I said. "Forget it. You did the right thing. Have a Coke.

We were sitting in the grill room again. The kid wasn't saying anything.

"Why didn't you throw that ball away?" I said.

"I don't know," the kid said. "I had the idea in my mind before he hit it, but I couldn't."

"Why?"

"I don't know why."

"I know why," I said.

The kid didn't say anything. He just sat there, looking down.

"Do you know why you couldn't throw that ball away?" I said.

"No," the kid said.

"You couldn't throw that ball away," I said, "because you're going to be a major-league ballplayer someday."

The kid just looked at me. He had that same sore expression.

"Do you know why you're going to be a major-league ballplayer?" I said.

Now it's time for YOU to be the Reader as Detective.

How did Harry Franklin know that Maneri would be a major-league ballplayer? Make your best guess. Read on to see if you are right.

The kid was just looking down again, shaking his head. I never got more of a kick out of anything in my life.

"You're going to be a major-league ballplayer," I said, "because you couldn't throw that ball away, and because I'm not Harry Franklin."

"What do you mean?" the kid said.

"I mean," I explained to him, "that I tried to needle you into throwing that ball away because I'm Eddie Brown."

Be a Reading Detective

Read each of the following questions. Then write the letter of the correct answer to each question. Remember, the symbol next to each question identifies the *kind* of reading skill that particular question helps you to develop.

1. Pete Maneri looked like
   a. Phil Rizzuto.
   b. Harry Franklin
   c. Eddie Brown.
   d. Nick the desk clerk.

2. Mr. Franklin said that he
   a. worked in a hotel.
   b. managed the Yankees.
   c. sold hardware.
   d. used to be a pitcher.

3. Harry Franklin tried to needle Pete into throwing the ball away. Which word or expression BEST defines the word *needle* as used in this context?

a. threaten
b. urge on
c. an instrument used in sewing
d. bribe

4. According to Maneri, Al Dall

    a. sent back good reports on him.
    b. bawled him out in front of everybody.
    c. was very friendly to him.
    d. respected him very much.

5. Probably, Franklin suggested that Maneri throw the ball away because he wanted

    a. the home team to lose the game.
    b. Maneri to make an error.
    c. to see if Maneri placed winning over personal gain.
    d. the game to be more exciting.

6. Which of the following is an opinion?

    a. Maneri led the league in stolen bases.
    b. Maneri was batting .365 in the minor leagues.
    c. Maneri is sure to lead the major leagues in batting one day.
    d. Maneri couldn't throw the ball away.

7. "I threw a couple of games away, and that really made the manager sore." Which of the following BEST defines the word *sore* as used in that sentence?

    a. angry
    b. depressed
    c. wounded
    d. cut

8. Which of the following is true of Maneri?

    a. He was a poor fielder.
    b. He lived in a rooming house.
    c. He had lots of speed.
    d. He got lots of mail.

9. Which happened last?

   a. The man at the desk introduced Pete to Mr. Franklin.

   b. Harry Franklin told Pete his real name.

   c. Maneri said he might throw a ball away.

   d. Pete and Harry Franklin had a drink together.

10. This story is mainly about

   a. how Pete Maneri made a bad throw and lost the game for his team.

   b. how a minor-league ballplayer proves himself to a big-league scout.

   c. how Eddie Brown checked into the Olympia Hotel on the main street in town.

   d. how Harry Franklin became a big-time baseball scout.

Follow the Trail

Story Clues

Did you realize that Harry Franklin was Eddie Brown? If so, when did you first suspect this? Answer the following questions. Each correct answer provides a story clue to the fact that Harry Franklin was Eddie Brown.

11. Which suggests that Harry Franklin was really a scout?

   a. He used to play baseball with Columbus.

   b. He enjoyed talking to Maneri.

   c. He heard that Maneri was angry at Al Dall.

   d. He waited for Maneri at the elevator.

12. Which is a clue that Franklin wasn't telling the truth about who he was?

   a. He said he made out route sheets and sales orders.

   b. He said he does some strange things.

   c. He could see that Maneri was madder than he'd said.

   d. He had a cup of coffee in the grill room.

13. During the game, Maneri "didn't have any hard chances." However, Franklin
    a. didn't mind coming back to see him another day.
    b. could see that he was a good ballplayer.
    c. thought the home team was outstanding.
    d. knew a chance would come.

14. Franklin had heard that Maneri was
    a. too good for his league.
    b. much taller than Rizzuto.
    c. not a very good fielder.
    d. angry about being yelled at.

15. Franklin told Maneri that he
    a. should try his best every game.
    b. should listen to his manager.
    c. was going to be a major-league ballplayer.
    d. shouldn't throw the ball away.

Notice how the correct answer to each question is a clue to the fact that Harry Franklin was a scout.

Find Word Meanings

The five words listed below appear in "One Throw." Study the words and their definitions. Use the page numbers to check how the words are used in the story. Then complete the following sentences by using each vocabulary word only *once*.

word	meaning	page
lobby	entrance hall	71
exaggerating	going beyond the truth	72
sore	angry; upset	74
career	life's work; way of living	74
bleachers	benches or stands for the fans at sporting events	74

It would not be overstating, or _____16_____ , to say that making it to the major leagues is a great accomplishment. Most baseball stars spend years in the minors first. There, they are given a lot of great opportunities to become better players. But life in the minors is difficult. There are long, tiring bus rides, and games played in front of _____17_____ that may contain only a hundred or so fans.

Living conditions in the minors are not very comfortable. Players spend lazy hours in their rooms or in the front _____18_____ of the hotel. And, of course, there are the _____19_____ and aching bones that come with playing almost every day. Still, players who hope for a _____20_____ in the major leagues are willing to put up with these conditions.

Look at Language

Figurative Language

Most of the time, authors use words according to their **literal**, or exact, dictionary definition. However, sometimes authors also use words **figuratively**. This means that they're using words in a more expressive or creative way, to help you picture something or to make an idea more memorable. For example, in the sentence "It's so cold in here that I'm frozen," the word *frozen* is used figuratively to express how cold the person is. The person is not *literally* turned to ice.

As Reader as Detective, you need to understand when an author is saying something figuratively. The following questions will give you practice identifying and interpreting figurative expressions.

21. Pete Maneri says, "He's on my neck all the time."

This means that Al Dall always

a. has his hands around Pete's neck.
b. stands too close to Pete.
c. picks on everything Pete does.
d. follows Pete around congratulating him.

22. When Pete says that Al Dall keeps "knocking" him down, he means that his coach keeps

   a. punching him to the floor.
   b. criticizing him and making him feel low.
   c. running into him on the field.
   d. taking him out of the game.

23. Which sentence contains a figurative expression?

   a. "It's not much of a ball park in this town—old wooden bleachers and an old wooden fence and about four hundred people in the stands."
   b. "Maybe you think this is mean to steam a kid up like this, but I do some strange things."
   c. "I could see from the way he said it that he was madder than he'd said."
   d. "The first game wasn't much of a game either, with the home club winning something like 8 to 1."

24. " 'Sure,' I said, egging him on."

   In this context, "egging him on" is a figurative expression meaning

   a. trying to get him to feel a certain way.
   b. attempting to cheer him up.
   c. tossing eggs at him.
   d. tricking him.

25. Which expression is figurative?

   a. " 'We'll keep an eye on you.' "
   b. " 'You're going to be a major-league ballplayer. . . .' "
   c. "I could see he didn't want to talk."
   d. " '. . . he's trying to keep you around.' "

Review the Case

The following activities will help you review and reflect on what happened in "One Throw."

1. Discuss. What do you think of the way Eddie Brown tested Pete Maneri? Should he have been honest about who he was instead? Why or why not?

2. **Write.** Life in the minor leagues is usually very lonely. Therefore, players call or write home frequently to receive and share news. Suppose Pete Maneri wrote a letter home describing what occurred with Mr. Franklin. What do you think he would say? Write Pete's letter. Address it to "Dear Folks." First write a rough draft of your letter. Proofread it carefully. Then write the final draft of your letter.

3. **Technology Application.** Pick an athlete from your favorite sport and look up the statistics for that person's performance over the past five years or so. Then create a graph that tracks the athlete's progress. Show your graph to the class and explain it.

**All I have is this one chance to get revenge,
and I'm grabbing it!**

I've Got Gloria

by M. E. Kerr

"Hello? Mrs. Whitman?"

"Yes?"

"I've got Gloria."

"Oh, thank heaven! Is she all right?"

"She's fine, Mrs. Whitman."

"Where is she?"

"She's here with me."

"Who are you?"

"You can call me Bud."

"Bud who?"

"Never mind that, Mrs. Whitman. I've got your little dog and she's anxious to get back home."

"Oh, I know she is. She must miss me terribly. Where are you? I'll come and get her right away."

"Not so fast, Mrs. Whitman. First, there's a little something you must do."

"Anything. Just tell me where to find you."

"*I'll* find *you*, Mrs. Whitman, *after* you do as I say."

"What do you mean, Bud?"

"I mean that I'll need some money before I get Gloria home safely to you."

"Money?"

"She's a very valuable dog."

"Not really. I got her from the pound."

"But she's valuable to you, isn't she?"

"She's everything to me."

"So you have to prove it, Mrs. Whitman."

"What is this?"

"A dognapping. I have your dog and you have to pay to have her returned safely to you."

There was a pause.

I could just imagine her face—that face I hated ever since she flunked me. That mean, freckled face, with the glasses over those hard little green eyes, the small, pursed lips, the mop of frizzy red hair topping it all. . . .Well, top this, Mrs. Whitman: I do not even have that nutsy little bulldog of yours. She *is* lost, just as your countless signs nailed up everywhere announce that she is. . . . All I have is this one chance to get revenge, and I'm grabbing it!

Now her voice came carefully. "How much do you want?"

"A thousand dollars, Mrs. Whitman. A thou, in one-hundred-dollars bills, and Gloria will be back drooling on your lap."

"A *thousand* dollars?"

Got to you, didn't I? Did your stomach turn over the way mine did when I saw that F in math?

"You heard me, Mrs. Whitman."

"Are you one of my students?"

"Oh, like I'm going to tell you if I am."

"You must be."

"I could be, couldn't I? You're not everyone's dream teacher, are you?"

"Please don't hurt my dog."

"I'm not cruel by nature."

I don't take after my old man. He said he was sorry that I flunked math because he knew how much I was counting on the hike through Yellowstone this summer. He said maybe the other guys would take some photographs so I could see what I was missing while I went to summer school to get a passing grade. "Gee, Scott," he said, "what a shame, and now you won't get an allowance, either, or have TV in your bedroom, or the use of the computer. But never mind, sonny boy," he said, "there'll be lots to do around the house. I'll leave lists for you every day of things to be done before I get home."

Mrs. Whitman whined, "I just don't have a thousand dollars. I don't know where I'll get so much money either."

Sometimes I whined that way, and my mom would say, "Scotty, we wouldn't be so hard on you if you'd only take responsibility for your actions. We tell you to be in at eleven P.M. and you claim the bus was late. We ask you to take the tapes back to Videoland and you say we never said to do it. You always have an excuse for everything! You never blame yourself!"

"Mrs. Whitman? I don't mean to be hard on you but that's the deal, see. A thou in hundreds."

"Just don't hurt Gloria."

"Gee, what a shame that you have to worry about such a thing. She's a sweet little dog, and I know she misses you because she's not eating."

"She doesn't eat dog food, Bud. I cook for her."

"That's why she doesn't eat, hmm? I don't know how to cook."

"You could just put a frozen dinner in the microwave. A turkey dinner, or a Swanson's pot roast. I'll pay you for it."

"A thousand dollars plus ten for frozen dinners? Is that what you're suggesting?"

"Let me think. Please. I have to think how I can get the money."

"Of course you do. I'll call you back, Mrs. Whitman, and meanwhile I'll go to the store and get some Swanson's frozen dinners."

"When will you—"

I hung up.

I could hear Dad coming up the stairs.

"Scott?"

"Yes, sir?"

"I'm going to take the Saturn in for an oil change. I want you to come with me."

"I have some homework, sir."

"I want you to come with me. Now."

———————◆———————

In the car, he said, "We need to talk."

"About what?" I said.

There was one of her Lost Dog signs tacked to the telephone pole at the end of our street.

"We need to talk about this summer," he said.

"What about it?"

"You *have* to make up the math grade. That you have to do. I'm sorry you can't go to Yellowstone."

"Yeah."

"There's no other way if you want to get into any kind of college. Your other grades are fine. But you need math. . . . What's so hard about math, Scott?"

"I hate it!"

"I did, too, but I learned it. You have to study."

"Mrs. Whitman doesn't like me."

"Why doesn't she like you?"

"She doesn't like anyone but that bulldog."

"Who's lost, apparently."

"Yeah."

"The signs are everywhere."

"Yeah."

"But she wouldn't deliberately flunk you, would she?"

"Who knows?"

"Do you really think a teacher would flunk you because she doesn't like you?"

"Who knows?"

"Scott, you've got to admit when you're wrong. I'll give you an example. I was wrong when I said you couldn't have an allowance or TV or use of the computer, et cetera. I was angry and I just blew! That was wrong. It wouldn't have made it any easier for you while you're trying to get a passing grade in math. So I was wrong. I apologize and I take it back."

"How come?"

"How come? Because I'm sorry. I thought about it and it bothered me. I'm a hothead, and I don't like that about myself. Okay?"

"Yeah."

"Maybe that's what's wrong here."

"What's wrong where?"

"Between us."

"Is something wrong between us?"

"Scotty, I'm trying to talk with you. About us, I want to work things out so we get along better."

"Yeah."

"Sometimes I do or say rash things."

"Yeah."

"I always feel lousy after."

"Oh, yeah?"

"Do you understand? I shouldn't take things out on you. That's petty. Life is hard enough. We don't have to be mean and spiteful with each other. Agreed?"

"Yeah." I was thinking about the time our dog didn't come home one night. I couldn't sleep. I even prayed. When he got back all muddy the next morning, I broke into tears and told him, "Now you're making me blubber like a baby!"

Dad was still on my case.

"Scott, I want you to think about why Mrs. Whitman flunked you."

"I just told you: she doesn't like me."

"Are you really convinced that you're good at math but the reason you failed was because she doesn't like you?"

"Maybe."

"Is she a good teacher?"

"She never smiles. She's got these tight little lips and these ugly freckles."

"So she's not a good teacher?"

"I can't learn from her."

"Did you study hard?"

"I studied. Sure. I studied."

"How many others flunked math?"

"What?"

"How many others flunked math?"

"No one."

"Speak up."

"I said, I'm the only one."

"So others learn from her despite her tight little lips and ugly freckles?"

"I guess."

"Scott, who's to blame for your flunking math?"

"Okay," I said. "Okay."

"Who is to blame?"

"Me. Okay? I didn't study that hard."

He sighed and said, "There. Good. You've accepted the blame. . . . How do you feel?"

"I feel okay." I really didn't, though. I was thinking about that dumb bulldog running loose somewhere, and about Mrs. Whitman worried sick now that she thought Gloria'd been dognapped.

Dad said, "I think we both feel a lot better."

———————◆———————

We sat around in the waiting room at Saturn.

Dad read *Sports Illustrated*, but I couldn't concentrate on the magazine there or the ball game on TV. I was down. I knew what Dad meant when he'd told me he felt bad after he "blew" and that he didn't like himself for it.

I kept glancing toward the pay phone. I stuck my hands in my pants pockets. I had a few quarters.

"I'm going to call Al and see what he's doing tonight," I said.

Dad said, "Wait until you get home. We'll be leaving here very shortly."

I didn't know Mrs. Whitman's number. I'd copied it down from one of the Lost Dog signs and ripped it up after I'd called her. I hadn't planned to follow up the call, get money from her: nothing like that. I just wanted to give her a good scare.

I went over to the phone book and looked her up.

Then I ducked inside the phone booth, fed the slot a quarter, and dialed.

"Hello?"

"Mrs. Whitman? I don't have your dog. I was playing a joke."

"I know you don't have my dog. Gloria's home. The dog warden found her and brought her back right after you hung up on me."

I was relieved. At least she wouldn't have to go all night worrying about getting Gloria back.

"I was wrong," I said. "It was petty. I'm sorry."

"Do you know what you put me through, Scott Perkins?"

I just hung up.

I stood there with my face flaming.

"Scott?" My father was looking all over for me, calling me and calling me. "Scott! Are you here? The car's ready!"

◆

All the way home he lectured me on how contrary I was. Why couldn't I have waited to phone Al? What was it about me that made me just go ahead and do something I was expressly told I shouldn't do? "Just when I think we've gotten someplace," he said, "you turn around and go against my wishes.

"*Why?*" he shouted.

I said, "What?" I hadn't been concentrating on all that he was saying. I was thinking that now she knew my name—don't ask me how—and now what was she going to do about it?

"I asked you *why* you go against my wishes," Dad said. "Nothing I say seems to register with you."

"It registers with me," I said. "I just seem to screw up sometimes."

"I can hardly believe my ears." He was smiling. "You actually said sometimes you screw up. That's a new one."

"Yeah," I said. "That's a new one."

Then we both laughed, but I was still shaking, remembering Mrs. Whitman saying my name that way.

When we got in the house, Mom said, "The funniest thing happened while you were gone. The phone rang and this woman asked what number this was. I told her, and she asked whom she was speaking to."

Now it's time for YOU to be the Reader as Detective.

Who do you think called, and what do you think the caller said?

"I told her and she said, 'Perkins . . . Perkins. Do you have a boy name Scott?' I said that we did . . . and she said, 'This is Martha Whitman. Tell him I'll see him this summer. I'm teaching remedial math.'"

I figured that right after I'd hung up from calling her about Gloria, she'd dialed *69. I'd heard you could do that. The phone would ring whoever called you last. That was why she'd asked my mother what number it was and who was speaking.

Dad said, "You see, Scott. Mrs. Whitman doesn't dislike you, or she wouldn't have called here to tell you she'd see you this summer."

"I was wrong," I said. "Wrong again."

Oh, was I ever!

Be a Reading Detective

Read each of the following questions. Then write the letter of the correct answer to each question. Remember, the symbol next to each question identifies the *kind* of reading skill that particular question helps you to develop.

1. Which event happened first?
   a. Gloria went missing.
   b. Scott called Mrs. Whitman.
   c. Scott's dad got an oil change.
   d. Scott was punished for failing math.

2. If Scott didn't actually have Mrs. Whitman's dog, how did he know it was lost?

   a. He saw lost dog signs.
   b. His father told him the dog was lost.
   c. A friend of his had the dog.
   d. Mrs. Whitman called Scott's house.

3. Which is a fact in the story?

   a. Scott calls his friend Al from the service station.
   b. Gloria does not eat dog food when she's home.
   c. Mrs. Whitman comes up with a thousand dollars.
   d. Scott's father won't let him use the phone all summer.

4. When Scott says, "I don't take after my old man" on page 85, at that point, he is most likely thinking that his father

   a. is being cruel about the summer.
   b. is good at math.
   c. is too nice to people.
   d. will get angry about the dognapping.

5. In the beginning of the story, Scott probably thinks that Mrs. Whitman is

   a. a careless pet owner.
   b. bad at math.
   c. a mean person.
   d. a terrible cook.

6. Which of these statements from the story is an opinion?

   a. "I don't have your dog."
   b. "She's a very valuable dog."
   c. "I got her from the pound."
   d. "Tell him I'll see him this summer."

7. Scott's dad says, "Sometimes I do or say *rash* things."

Here, *rash* probably means

a. angry.
b. silly.
c. without thinking.
d. wrong.

8. Which is *not* an example that Scott's parents give to show Scott is irresponsible?

a. They say Scott doesn't return videotapes.
b. They say Scott comes home too late.
c. They say Scott shouldn't have called Mrs. Whitman.
d. They say Scott failed math because he didn't work hard enough.

9. What happened after Scott and his dad left the house to get an oil change?

a. Scott's father noticed the lost dog signs.
b. Mrs. Whitman called Scott back.
c. Scott went to the store to buy TV dinners.
d. Scott's mom came up the stairs.

10. This story makes the point that

a. teachers have too much power over students' lives.
b. people should accept responsibility for their actions.
c. people should be more careful not to let their pets wander off.
d. parents and children often don't get along.

Follow the Trail

Characters

To fully enjoy and appreciate what you are reading, you must recognize and understand the characters' different personalities and beliefs. In "I've Got Gloria," for example, Scott's personality plays an important part in the story. The following questions will help you think about characters.

11. Which is true of Scott's dad?

    a. He is too nice and never punishes Scott.

    b. He is stubborn and never admits when he's wrong.

    c. He overreacts but admits it.

    d. He is not involved in Scott's life.

12. On page 88, how does Scott feel after admitting he just didn't study?

    a. guilty

    b. relieved

    c. angry

    d. proud

13. How does Scott's mom feel about his behavior?

    a. She thinks Scott is too hard on himself.

    b. She thinks that Scott's dad is too hard on him.

    c. She thinks that Scott is too easy on himself.

    d. She thinks that Scott is the perfect son.

14. Compare Scott and his dad.

    a. Both overreact to problems but then realize they were wrong.

    b. Scott always overreacts, and his dad always stays calm.

    c. Scott's dad always overreacts, and Scott stays calm.

    d. They are both calm in the face of problems.

15. What does Scott learn at the end of the story?

    a. Mrs. Whitman is as mean as he thought.

    b. He'll be able to go on vacation after all.

    c. He needs to be sneakier the next time he fakes a dognapping.

    d. He should have studied for the math test.

Find Word Meanings

The five words listed below appear in "I've Got Gloria." Study the words and their definitions. Use the page numbers to check how the words are used in the story. Then complete the following sentences by using each vocabulary word only *once*.

word	meaning	page
deliberately	on purpose; intending to do	86
despite	even though	88
contrary	going against; disagreeing with, or disobeying	89
expressly	specifically	89
remedial	meant to improve or correct	90

Like Scott from "I've Got Gloria," I used to dislike math. My teacher, Mr. Johnson, constantly offered to give me _____16_____ lessons after school, but I refused. Mr. Johnson did his best to help me, but _____17_____ all of his effort, I was stubborn and _____18_____, always doing the opposite of what he said. Whenever I had homework, I'd blow it off and watch TV instead. If my parents asked how my homework was coming, I'd _____19_____ lie and pretend I had finished it. Whenever I did poorly on a test, I'd lie and say that my teacher never told us what would be on the test, even if he had _____20_____ told us what to study. Then one day, my soccer coach warned me that if I got an F in any of my classes, I wouldn't be able to play on the team anymore. After that incident, I began trying harder in math. And I ended up enjoying it more than I thought!

Look at Language

Context Clues

Often, you can figure out the meaning of a difficult or unfamiliar word by looking at the *context*—the words (and sometimes the sentences) around the word. **Context clues** will help you find the word's meaning.

As the Reader as Detective, you have already had experience using vocabulary clues to figure out word meanings. The following questions will provide additional practice in using context clues to find the word's meaning.

21. " 'We tell you to be in at eleven P.M. and you claim the bus was late.' " *Claim* most likely means

  a. state to be true.
  b. lie unconvincingly.
  c. scream loudly.
  d. state convincingly.

22. " 'I shouldn't take things out on you. That's petty. Life is hard enough. We don't have to be mean and spiteful with each other.' " In this context, *spiteful* means to be filled with

  a. regret for the problems you've caused.
  b. hatred or the desire to cause someone pain.
  c. desire to ignore someone.
  d. sadness over the pains of life.

23. " 'The dog warden found her and brought her back right after you hung up on me.' " A *warden* is a

  a. hunter.
  b. a guardian or keeper.
  c. veterinarian.
  d. owner.

24. " 'Now you're making me blubber like a baby!' " In this context, *blubber* most likely means

  a. chubby like a whale.
  b. cry heavily.
  c. scream with anger.
  d. turn red with embarrassment.

25. " 'It registers with me,' I said. 'I just seem to screw up sometimes.' " To *register* something means to

a. spend money for it.
b. note or understand it.
c. deny it.
d. misunderstand it.

Review the Case

The following activities will help you review and reflect on what happened in "I've Got Gloria."

1. Discuss. What do you think of Scott's pretending to have kidnapped Mrs. Whitman's dog? Did he overreact? Was he justified? In other words, did he have good reason to play the prank on Mrs. Whitman?

2. Write. Think back to a memorable teacher. Describe him or her in detail, making sure to explain why he or she was so memorable.

3. Technology Application. Use creative tools on your home, school, or library computer to make a missing pet poster. (It doesn't have to be a cat or dog.) Add pictures and use fonts that will attract attention.

**It was probably at that precise moment that
the Moose decided to go public.**

Just Once

by Thomas J. Dygard

Everybody liked the Moose. To his father and mother he was
Bryan—as in Bryan Jefferson Crawford—but to everyone at
Bedford City High he was the Moose. He was large and strong, as
you might imagine from the nickname, and he was pretty fast on
his feet—sort of nimble, you might say—considering his size. He
didn't have a pretty face but he had a quick and easy smile—
"sweet," some of the teachers called it; "nice," others said.

But on the football field, the Moose was neither sweet nor nice.
He was just strong and fast and a little bit devastating as the left
tackle of the Bedford City Bears. When the Moose blocked somebody, he stayed blocked. When the Moose was called on to open
a hole in the line for one of the Bears' runners, the hole more often
than not resembled an open garage door.

Now in his senior season, the Moose had twice been named to
the all-conference team and was considered a cinch for all-state. He
spent a lot of his spare time, when he wasn't in a classroom or on
the football field, reading letters from colleges eager to have the
Moose pursue higher education—and football—at their institution.

But the Moose had a hang-up.

He didn't go public with his hang-up until the sixth game of the
season. But, looking back, most of his teammates agreed that probably the Moose had been nurturing the hang-up secretly for two
years or more.

The Moose wanted to carry the ball.

For sure, the Moose was not the first interior lineman in the history of football, or even the history of Bedford City High, who banged heads up front and wore bruises like badges of honor—and dreamed of racing down the field with the ball to the end zone while everybody in the bleachers screamed his name.

But most linemen, it seems, are able to stifle the urge. The idea may pop into their minds from time to time, but in their hearts they know they can't run fast enough, they know they can't do that fancy dancing to elude tacklers, they know they aren't trained to read blocks. They know that their strength and talents are best utilized in the line. Football is, after all, a team sport, and everyone plays the position where he most helps the team. And so these linemen,  or most of them, go back to banging heads without saying the first word about the dream that flickered through their minds.

Not so with the Moose.

That sixth game, when the Moose's hang-up first came into public view, had ended with the Moose truly in all his glory as the Bears' left tackle. Yes, glory—but uncheered and sort of anonymous. The Bears were trailing 21–17 and had the ball on Mitchell High's five-yard line, fourth down, with time running out. The rule in such a situation is simple—the best back carries the ball behind the best blocker—and it is a rule seldom violated by those in control of their faculties. The Bears, of course, followed the rule. That meant Jerry Dixon running behind the Moose's blocking. With the snap of the ball, the Moose knocked down one lineman, bumped another one aside, and charged forward to flatten an approaching linebacker. Jerry did a little jig behind the Moose and then ran into the end zone, virtually untouched, to win the game.

After circling in the end zone a moment while the cheers echoed through the night, Jerry did run across and hug the Moose, that's true. Jerry knew who had made the touchdown possible.

But it wasn't the Moose's name that everybody was shouting. The fans in the bleachers were cheering Jerry Dixon.

It was probably at that precise moment that the Moose decided to go public.

In the dressing room, Coach Buford Williams was making his rounds among the cheering players and came to a halt in front of the Moose. "It was your great blocking that did it," he said.

"I want to carry the ball," the Moose said.

Coach Williams was already turning away and taking a step toward the next player due an accolade when his brain registered the fact that the Moose had said something strange. He was expecting the Moose to say, "Aw, gee, thanks, Coach." That was what the Moose always said when the coach issued a compliment. But the Moose had said something else. The coach turned back to the Moose, a look of disbelief on his face. "What did you say?"

"I want to carry the ball," the Moose said.

Coach Williams was good at quick recoveries, as any high-school football coach had better be. He gave a tolerant smile and a little nod and said, "You keep right on blocking, son."

This time Coach Williams made good on his turn and moved away from the Moose.

The following week's practice and the next Friday's game passed without further incident. After all, the game was a road game over at Cartwright High, thirty-five miles away. The Moose wanted to carry the ball in front of the Bedford City fans.

Then the Moose went to work.

He caught up with the coach on the way to the practice field on Wednesday. "Remember," he said, leaning forward and down a little to get his face in the coach's face, "I said I want to carry the ball."

Coach Williams must have been thinking about something else because it took him a minute to look up into the Moose's face, and even then he didn't say anything.

"I meant it," the Moose said.

"Meant what?"

"I want to run the ball."

"Oh," Coach Williams said. Yes, he remembered. "Son, you're a great left tackle, a great blocker. Let's leave it that way."

The Moose let the remaining days of the practice week and then the game on Friday night against Edgewood High pass while he reviewed strategies. The review led him to Dan Blevins, the Bears' quarterback. If the signal-caller would join in, maybe Coach Williams would listen.

"Yeah, I heard," Dan said. "But, look, what about Joe Wright at guard, Bill Slocum at right tackle, even Herbie Watson at center. They might all want to carry the ball. What are we going to do—take turns? It doesn't work that way."

So much for Dan Blevins.

The Moose found that most of the players in the backfield agreed with Dan. They couldn't see any reason why the Moose should carry the ball, especially in place of themselves. Even Jerry Dixon, who owed a lot of his glory to the Moose's blocking, gaped in disbelief at the Moose's idea. The Moose, however, got some support from his fellow linemen. Maybe they had dreams of their own, and saw value in a precedent.

As the days went by, the word spread—not just on the practice field and in the corridors of Bedford City High, but all around town. The players by now were openly taking sides. Some thought it a jolly good idea that the Moose carry the ball. Others, like Dan Blevins, held to the purist line—a left tackle plays left tackle, a ball-carrier carries the ball, and that's it.

Around town, the vote wasn't even close. Everyone wanted the Moose to carry the ball.

"Look, son," Coach Williams said to the Moose on the practice field the Thursday before the Benton Heights game, "this has gone far enough. Fun is fun. A joke is a joke. But let's drop it."

"Just once," the Moose pleaded.

Coach Williams looked at the Moose and didn't answer.

The Moose didn't know what that meant.

The Benton Heights Tigers were duck soup for the Bears, as everyone knew they would be. The Bears scored in their first three possessions and led 28–0 at the half. The hapless Tigers had yet to cross the fifty-yard line under their own steam.

All the Bears, of course, were enjoying the way the game was going, as were the Bedford City fans jamming the bleachers.

Coach Williams looked irritated when the crowd on a couple of occasions broke into a chant: "Give the Moose the ball! Give the Moose the ball!"

On the field, the Moose did not know whether to grin at hearing his name shouted by the crowd or to frown because the sound of his name was irritating the coach. Was the crowd going to talk Coach Williams into putting the Moose in the backfield? Probably not; Coach Williams didn't bow to that kind of pressure. Was the coach going to refuse to give the ball to the Moose just to show the crowd—and the Moose and the rest of the players—who was boss? The Moose feared so.

In his time on the sideline, when the defensive unit was on the field, the Moose, of course, said nothing to Coach Williams. He knew better than to break the coach's concentration during a game—even a runaway victory—with a comment on any subject at all, much less his desire to carry the ball. As a matter of fact, the Moose was careful to stay out of the coach's line of vision, especially when the crowd was chanting "Give the Moose the ball!"

By the end of the third quarter the Bears were leading 42–0.

Now it's time for YOU to be the Reader as Detective.

Do you think Coach Williams will give the Moose the ball? Explain.

Keep reading to see what Coach Williams decides.

Coach Williams had been feeding substitutes into the game since halftime, but the Bears kept marching on. And now, in the opening minutes of the fourth quarter, the Moose and his teammates were standing on the Tigers' five-yard line, about to pile on another touchdown.

The Moose saw his substitute, Larry Hinden, getting a slap on the behind and then running onto the field. The Moose turned to leave.

Then he heard Larry tell the referee, "Hinden for Holbrook."

Holbrook? Chad Holbrook, the fullback?

Chad gave the coach a funny look and jogged off the field.

Larry joined the huddle and said, "Coach says the Moose at fullback and give him the ball."

Dan Blevins said, "Really?"

"Really."

The Moose was giving his grin—"sweet," some of the teachers called it; "nice," others said.

"I want to do an end run," the Moose said.

Dan looked at the sky a moment, then said, "What does it matter?"

The quarterback took the snap from center, moved back and to his right while turning, and extended the ball to the Moose.

The Moose took the ball and cradled it in his right hand. So far, so good. He hadn't fumbled. Probably both Coach Williams and Dan were surprised.

He ran a couple of steps and looked out in front and said aloud, "Whoa!"

Where had all those tacklers come from?"

The whole world seemed to be peopled with players in red jerseys—the red of the Benton Heights Tigers. They all were look-ing straight at the Moose and advancing toward him. They looked very determined, and not friendly at all. And there were so many of them. The Moose had faced tough guys in the line, but usually one at a time, or may two. But this—five or six. And all of them heading for him.

The Moose screeched to a halt, whirled, and ran the other way.

Dan Blevins blocked somebody in a red jersey breaking through the middle of the line, and the Moose wanted to stop running and thank him. But he kept going.

His reverse had caught the Tigers' defenders going the wrong way, and the field in front of the Moose looked open. But his block-ers were going the wrong way, too. Maybe that was why the field looked so open. What did it matter, though, with the field clear in front of him? This was going to be a cakewalk; the Moose was going to score a touchdown.

Then, again—"Whoa!"

Players with red jerseys were beginning to fill the empty space—a lot of them. And they were all running toward the Moose. They were kind of low, with their arms spread, as if they wanted to hit him hard and them grab him.

A picture of Jerry Dixon dancing his little jig and wriggling between tacklers flashed through the Moose's mind. How did Jerry do that? Well, no time to ponder that one right now.

The Moose lowered his shoulder and thundered ahead, into the cloud of red jerseys. Something hit his left thigh. It hurt. Then something pounded his hip, then his shoulder. They both hurt. Somebody was hanging on to him and was a terrible drag. How could he run with somebody hanging on to him? He knew he was going down, but maybe he was across the goal. He hit the ground hard, with somebody coming down on top of him, right on the small of his back.

The Moose couldn't move. They had him pinned. Wasn't the referee supposed to get these guys off?

Finally the load was gone and the Moose, still holding the ball, got to his knees and one hand, then stood.

He heard the screaming of the crowd, and he saw the scoreboard blinking.

He had scored.

His teammates were slapping him on the shoulder pads and laughing and shouting.

The Moose grinned, but he had a strange and distant look in his eyes.

He jogged to the sideline, the roars of the crowd still ringing in his ears.

"Okay, son?" Coach Williams asked.

The Moose was puffing. He took a couple of deep breaths. He relived for a moment the first sight of a half dozen players in red jerseys, all with one target—him. He saw again the menacing horde of red jerseys that had risen up just when he'd thought he had clear sailing to the goal. They all zeroed in on him, the Moose alone.

The Moose glanced at the coach, took another deep breath, and said, "Never again."

Be a Reading Detective

Read each of the following questions. Then write the letter of the correct answer to each question. Remember, the symbol next to each question identifies the *kind* of reading skill that particular question helps you to develop.

1. This story is mainly about
   a. how well somebody can play football.
   b. the glory of playing sports at a high level.
   c. somebody learning the value of teamwork.
   d. finding out that we all have limitations.

2. "When the Moose was called on to open a hole in the line for one of the Bears' runners, the hole more often than not resembled an open garage door."

As used in this context, the word *resembled* most likely means

a. looked like.
b. worked as if.
c. blocked like.
d. was as strong as.

3. What did Jerry Dixon do after he scored the touchdown against Mitchell High?

a. He told the Moose he could not carry the ball.
b. He gave the Moose a hug to thank him.
c. He did a little jig as a victory dance.
d. He told the crowd they should cheer for the Moose.

4. Why would the Moose want to carry the ball in front of Bedford City fans?

a. He feels more comfortable at home.
b. He thinks he has a better chance in Bedford City.
c. He wants to hear his hometown cheering for him.
d. He wants to show his opponents what he can do.

5. In a close game like the one on page 98, why is the rule to have the best runner carry the ball behind the best blocker?

a. That gives the team the best chances of winning.
b. The coach wouldn't want his best runner to get hurt.
c. This is the strategy used by professional teams.
d. This will get the crowd to cheer for both the runner and the blocker.

6. What opinion did most of the people in town have of the Moose's idea?

   a. They didn't want the Bears to lose a game.
   b. They liked Jerry Dixon as the running back.
   c. They thought the Moose was a very nice boy.
   d. They thought he should be allowed to carry the ball.

7. To get what he wanted, what did the Moose do first?

   a. He asked the quarterback.
   b. He talked to the coach.
   c. He put the word out in town.
   d. He worked hard at practice.

8. Which position does Dan Blevins play on the team?

   a. punter
   b. right tackle
   c. quarterback
   d. running back

9. "Coach Williams was already turning away and taking a step toward the next player due on accolade. . . ." Based on the context of this sentence from page 99, *accolade* means a

   a. compliment or expression of praise.
   b. harsh critique.
   c. funny remark.
   d. strict warning.

10. "How did Jerry do that? Well, no time to ponder that one right now."

    What is another way to say *ponder* in this context?

    a. try to do
    b. see
    c. think about
    d. enjoy

Follow the Trail

Inferences

When you make an **inference** about something, you state an opinion or observation based on information in the text and your own knowledge. An active reader makes inferences about characters and events in a story. The following questions will help you practice this skill.

11. At the end of the story, why does the Moose have a strange and distant look in his eyes?

    a. He is angry at his coach.
    b. He feels scared and shaken up.
    c. He is thinking about college.
    d. He is angry about the touchdown.

12. What might the Moose have learned from the townspeople's reaction to his idea, even if he didn't get to carry the ball?

    a. They loved and supported him as a player.
    b. He should stick to the position he usually plays.
    c. He should just take the ball and run with it.
    d. They thought he should realize it was just a game.

13. Why does a picture of Jerry Dixon doing his little jig flash through the Moose's mind on page 102?

    a. The Moose is trying to figure out how to do it.
    b. The Moose is starting to realize each player has a different job.
    c. The Moose always thinks of Jerry Dixon when he plays.
    d. The Moose is excited about getting the cheers Jerry Dixon usually gets.

14. In future games, the Moose will probably

    a. wish he could run the ball again.
    b. be happy playing as a blocker.
    c. learn how to dodge other players.
    d. not count on the quarterback's support.

15. After high school, the Moose will most likely
    a. request to carry the ball in college.
    b. have trouble getting into college.
    c. play tackle for his college team.
    d. play both positions on his college team.

Find Word Meanings

The five words listed below appear in "Just Once." Study the words and their definitions. Use the page numbers to check how the words are used in the story. Then complete the following sentences by using each vocabulary word only *once*.

word	meaning	page
stifle	keep covered or unknown; push down	98
elude	avoid	98
faculties	mental powers or abilities	98
tolerant	understanding; putting up with	99
hapless	unlucky; lacking ability	100

The story "Just Once" reminds many people of their own experiences in school. Even if you've never played football, you can probably relate to what the Moose goes through. Who hasn't wanted to try something different in the hope of gaining attention and popularity?

When I was in school, I played the flute, but deep down, I wanted to play the drums instead. I tried to _____16_____ my desire, because I was afraid my music teacher would laugh at me. She might think that I lost my _____17_____ or something. After all, the drummers at my school were usually the popular boys, and I was a shy, quiet girl. For a while, I would _____18_____ her in the halls, because I didn't want her to see me and ask how I was liking the flute. I didn't know if I could tell her the truth.

One day, I finally decided to be bold and tell her about my dream of playing the drums. She was surprisingly _____19_____ of my idea, and she agreed to let me try them. I figured I'd be a _____20_____ drummer, but I ended up being good at it, and I switched for rest of the year! I even joined a rock band that met after school.

Look at Language

Descriptive Language

Writers use vivid, **descriptive language** to bring a story alive for readers. For example, saying that the Moose "screeched to a halt" is a lot more powerful than just saying that the Moose "stopped." The word *screeched* helps you understand that he stopped short and imagine the sound that he made.

Answer the following questions about descriptive language in "Just Once."

21. "When the Moose was called on to open a hole in the line for one of the Bears' runners, the hole more often than not resembled an open garage door."

    The author uses the image of an open garage door to show how the Moose

    a. did a decent job clearing a hole in the line.
    b. went above and beyond as a tackler.
    c. couldn't make the right kind of football formation.
    d. failed to create enough space for the runners.

22. "And so these linemen, or most of them, go back to banging heads without saying the first word about the dream that flickered through their minds."

    The phrase "flickered through their minds" shows that for most linemen, the idea of carrying the ball was a

    a. dream they had every day and night.
    b. thought that came and went quickly.
    c. thought that never dawned on them.
    d. goal that would stay with them forever.

23. "Coach Williams was already turning away and taking a step toward the next player due an accolade when his brain registered the fact that the Moose had said something strange."

The phrase "his brain registered the fact" shows that the coach had

a. a way of forgetting things people said.
b. a delayed reaction to the Moose's comment.
c. an angry reaction to the Moose's comment.
d. an immediate response to the Moose's comment.

24. "Coach Williams was good at quick recoveries, as any high-school football coach had better be. He gave a tolerant smile and a little nod and said, 'You keep right on blocking, son.'"

The author describes the coach's *tolerant* smile to show that he was

a. supportive of the Moose's dream.
b. laughing and smirking at the Moose.
c. willing to put up with the Moose.
d. impatient with the Moose's demands.

25. "The Moose lowered his shoulder and thundered ahead, into the cloud of red jerseys."

The author uses this image to show that the Moose

a. was a powerful force on the field.
b. made a lot of noise on the field.
c. played in a dreamlike, heavenly way.
d. had to face bad weather on game day.

Review the Case

The following activities will help you review and reflect on what happened in "Just Once."

1. Discuss. In many areas of life, there are "unsung heroes," people who do a lot of work but who are not recognized for their efforts. Give some examples of people like this and talk about how they might get more recognition for what they do.

2. **Write.**   Write an article about the final game between the Bears and the Tigers. Write as though you are a sports reporter for the school newspaper who was at the game and saw exactly what happened.

3. **Technology Application.**   If you're not familiar with football, there may have been parts of the story about the game that were confusing. Find an online video, on a site like YouTube, that clearly explains the rules of football. Then read the story again to see if the parts about football make more sense.

> At the doorway, De Ville turned his head. He
> shot a swift look back at his enemy. The look
> troubled me at the time. For not only did I see
> hatred in it, I saw triumph as well.

The Leopard Man's Story

by Jack London

He had a dreamy, faraway look in his eyes, and his voice was soft and gentle. He was thin and pale, and he seemed very sad. He was the Leopard Man, though he did not look it.

He earned his living working at a circus. Every day he climbed into a cage filled with leopards. He thrilled vast audiences with his skill and nerve. For this he was well paid.

For an hour I had been trying to get a story out of him. But he could think of nothing to tell me. He did not consider his work dangerous or daring. He did not think it thrilling. To him it was a job, one that sometimes became boring.

"How about lions?" I asked.

"Oh yes," he said. "I have often fought with them. But it is nothing. All one must do is stay alert. Anyone can whip a lion with an ordinary stick. I fought one for half an hour once. Just hit him on the nose every time he rushed. That was all."

He showed me his scars. There were many of them. I saw a recent one. A tiger had clawed his shoulder and cut him to the bone. His right arm, from his elbow down, was filled with old wounds. "It is nothing," he said. "Only they sometimes bother me when the rainy weather comes."

Suddenly his face brightened with a recollection. For he was really as eager to give me a story as I was to get one.

"Let me tell you about a fellow I knew. He was a little, thin, sword-swallowing knife-thrower. He called himself De Ville. Now this De Ville had a quick temper, as quick as his hand; and his hand was as quick as the paw of a tiger.

"One day the ringmaster called De Ville a name. De Ville shoved him against the wooden board that he used in his knife-throwing act. He did it so quickly, the ringmaster didn't have time to think. There, in front of the audience, De Ville filled the air with knives. He sunk them into the wood all around the ringmaster. They were so close that they passed through his clothes and just touched his skin. The clowns had to pull out the knives to get him loose. So the word went around the circus to watch out for De Ville.

"But there was one man, Wallace, who was afraid of nothing—not even De Ville. Wallace was the lion tamer. He used to put his head into the mouth of a lion. Any lion would do. But he preferred Augustus, a big, good-natured beast.

"As I was saying, Wallace—'King' Wallace we called him—was afraid of nothing. He really was a king, make no mistake about it. I saw him, on a wager, go into the cage of a lion that had turned nasty. Without a stick Wallace beat that lion. Just did it with his fist."

The Leopard Man paused. He looked thoughtfully at a sick lion in a nearby cage. Then he continued.

"One day 'King' Wallace and De Ville got into a fight. Wallace picked up De Ville and dropped him into a bucket of water. Then laughing at him, Wallace walked away.

"De Ville was soaked. He must have been furious. But he stayed cool as a cucumber and made no threat at all. However, I saw a glitter in his eyes which I had often seen in the eyes of wild beasts. I warned Wallace, but he only laughed at me.

"Several months passed by. Nothing had happened and I was beginning to think it was a scare over nothing. By that time we had arrived out West in San Francisco. The afternoon show was going on, and the big tent was filled. I was looking for Red Denny, who had walked off with my pocket-knife.

"As I walked past one of the dressing tents, I glanced through a hole in the canvas to see if I could find him. Red Denny wasn't there. But right in front of me was 'King' Wallace. He was waiting to go on with his lions.

"Wallace was watching with amusement a quarrel between two acrobats. Everyone was looking at them closely—all except De Ville. He was staring with undisguised hatred at Wallace. They were all too busy to notice what happened next. But I saw it through the hole in the canvas.

"De Ville carefully took his handkerchief from his pocket. He made believe he was wiping the sweat from his face with it, for it was a very hot day. Then he began to walk toward the exit of the tent. As he brushed by behind Wallace's back, he shook out the handkerchief. At the doorway, De Ville turned his head. He shot a swift look back at his enemy. The look troubled me at the time. For not only did I see hatred in it, I saw triumph as well.

" 'I must watch De Ville,' I said to myself. And I breathed easier when I saw him leave the circus grounds.

"A few minutes later, I found Red Denny in the big tent. 'King' Wallace's act had just begun. He was in particularly good form and was keeping the audience spellbound. He kept all the lions stirred up, snarling and growling around him. All of them, that is, except old Augustus. He was just too fat and too lazy to get excited about anything.

"Finally Wallace cracked his whip to get the old lion into position. Augustus blinked good-naturedly and opened his mouth. In went Wallace's head. Then the jaws came together, crunch, just like that."

The Leopard Man smiled in a sorrowful way, and the faraway look came into his eyes.

"And that was the end of 'King' Wallace," he went on in a sad, low voice. "After the excitement cooled down I watched my chance. I bent over and smelled Wallace's head. Then I sneezed."

"It . . . it was . . . ?" I asked, eager to know.

Now it's time for YOU to be the Reader as Detective.

What do you think the Leopard Man answered?

Think back to the story before you answer. Then read on to see if you are right.

"Pepper—that De Ville dropped on his hair in the dressing tent. Old Augustus never meant to do it. He just sneezed."

Be a Reading Detective

Read each of the following questions. Then write the letter of the correct answer to each question. Remember, the symbol next to each question identifies the *kind* of reading skill that particular question helps you to develop.

1. The Leopard Man thought that his job was
   a. very dangerous.
   b. thrilling.
   c. sometimes boring.
   d. entertaining.

2. "King" Wallace was afraid of
   a. Augustus.
   b. De Ville.
   c. nobody.
   d. Red Denny.

3. Which happened first?

   a. The ringmaster called De Ville a name.
   b. Everyone watched a quarrel between two acrobats.
   c. Wallace dropped De Ville into a bucket of water.
   d. The clowns pulled out the knives.

4. Leopard Man "glanced through a hole in the canvas." As used in this sentence, what is the meaning of the word *glanced*?

   a. hit sharply
   b. looked quickly
   c. flashed with light
   d. cut open

5. What did De Ville do to the ringmaster?

   a. He shoved him against a wooden board.
   b. He threw knives close to him.
   c. both of the above.
   d. none of the above.

6. You can infer that De Ville

   a. sprinkled some pepper onto his handkerchief.
   b. was not really angry at Wallace.
   c. had not worked at the circus very long.
   d. was generally a happy person.

7. Which of the following is a fact?

   a. It is more fun to go to the circus than to go to a ball game.
   b. The Leopard Man was usually very cheerful.
   c. The Leopard Man had old and recent scars from his work.
   d. Wallace got what he deserved.

8. On a wager, "King" Wallace went into the cage of a lion that had turned nasty. Which of the following BEST defines the word *wager*?

   a. wish
   b. bet
   c. small wagon
   d. adventure

9. After Wallace's death, which of the following is probably true?

   a. De Ville was sorry for what he had done.
   b. The Leopard Man grew to fear animals.
   c. The circus closed forever.
   d. De Ville continued working with lions.

10. Which sentence BEST gives the main idea of the story?

    a. A circus performer gets even with his enemy.
    b. Working in a circus can be very dangerous.
    c. Most old lions are fat and lazy.
    d. Lion tamers have exciting jobs.

Follow the Trail

Story Clues

As you've learned, story clues are hints or signposts that point the way to how the story will end. How good a reading detective were you? Did you spot the story clues in "The Leopard Man's Story"?

Think about the story. Then answer the following questions. Each is based on a story clue found in the selection.

11. The following sentences appear in "The Leopard Man's Story." Which one suggests how De Ville will get revenge on Wallace?

    a. " 'But [De Ville] stayed as cool as a cucumber and made no threat at all.' "

    b. " 'The afternoon show was going on, and the big tent was filled.' "

    c. " 'De Ville had a quick temper, as quick as his hand; and his hand was as quick as the paw of a tiger.' "

    d. " 'I warned Wallace, but he only laughed at me.' "

12. De Ville put pepper on Wallace's head when he

    a. "brushed by behind Wallace's back" and "shook out the handkerchief."

    b. "shoved him against the wooden board."

    c. "filled the air with knives."

    d. "was staring with undisguised hatred at Wallace."

13. The reader should be suspicious about the handkerchief because De Ville

    a. used it on a hot day.

    b. hid the handkerchief in his pocket.

    c. walked toward the exit with it.

    d. shook it out right behind Wallace.

14. The Leopard Man was afraid of what De Ville might do because De Ville

    a. warned Wallace to stay away from him.

    b. had in his eyes the glitter of a wild beast.

    c. was very friendly with the acrobats.

    d. was a knife swallower.

15. The reader should realize that De Ville had succeeded in his plan when he

    a. shot a look of triumph at his enemy.

    b. saw Wallace watching a quarrel.

    c. stared at Wallace with hatred.

    d. left the dressing tent.

Review your answers to the questions above. Notice how they provide clues to how the story will end.

Find Word Meanings

The five words listed below appear in "The Leopard Man's Story." Study the words and their definitions. Use the page numbers to check how the words are used in the story. Then complete the following sentences by using each vocabulary word only *once*.

word	meaning	page
vast	very great	111
recollection	memory	112
undisguised	not hidden; open	113
triumph	success; victory	113
eager	enthusiastic and impatient	114

The stories and novels of Jack London have excited and thrilled a _____16_____ number of readers. After reading one London story, you'll probably be _____17_____ to read another one.

Many of London's works are obviously based on actual, and _____18_____ , events that he experienced during his lifetime. For the plots of his novels, for example, London often drew upon his memory, or _____19_____ , of his days as a sailor.

As a writer, London experienced _____20_____ and success. He produced numerous short stories, novels, and political essays, many of which are still widely read today.

Look at Language

Compound Words

A **compound word** is a word that is made up of two smaller words. For example, *table* and *cloth* combine to form the compound word *tablecloth*. Other examples of compound words are *campfire*, *flashlight*, and *skyscraper*. Often, you can figure out the meaning of a difficult compound word by combining the meanings of the two smaller words.

The following questions will help you understand compound words in "The Leopard Man's Story."

21. The compound word *ringmaster* means

    a. a performer who tames lions.

    b. the person in charge of a circus performance.

    c. somebody who trains acrobats.

    d. anyone who is a natural storyteller.

22. Which is *not* a compound word?

    a. faraway

    b. sometimes

    c. doorway

    d. thoughtfully

23. As used on page 113, the compound word *spellbound* means

    a. under a magic spell or trance

    b. tied up to something

    c. motionless with fright

    d. too interested to move

24. Which of these expressions from the story contains a compound word?

    a. the afternoon show

    b. brushed by behind

    c. keeping the audience

    d. in a sorrowful way

25. Identify the compound word in the following list from the story.

    a. continued

    b. dressing

    c. anyone

    d. amusement

Review the Case

The following activities will help you review and reflect on what happened in "The Leopard Man's Story."

1. **Discuss.** Both the Leopard Man and King Wallace work with animals in the circus. In what ways are they alike, and in what ways are they different?

2. **Write.** Pretend that you are the Leopard Man. Write a one-page witness report about what you saw the night that Wallace was killed. Describe how De Ville acted, what seemed suspicious to you, etc. Later, read your report to the class.

3. **Technology Application.** Why does pepper make people sneeze? Using electronic research sources (the Internet, encyclopedias on CD-ROM, library databases), find out what pepper does inside a person's nose that causes sneezing. Compare your results with those of your classmates.

"I have learned that something of the greatest importance has been purloined—yes, *stolen*—from an office in the royal palace."

The Purloined Letter

PART I

by Edgar Allan Poe

In Paris, one windy evening, I was visiting my good friend, the world-famous detective, C. Auguste Dupin. Our conversation was interrupted by a loud knocking on the door. Dupin threw it open. There stood Mr. Gerrard, the chief of the Paris police.

We gave him a hearty welcome, for he was a delightful old friend whom we had not seen for many years.

"I am sorry to trouble you," said Gerrard. Here he turned to Dupin. "But I would like to ask your opinion about a recent case. It has been causing me a great deal of trouble."

"Please have a seat," said Dupin. He pointed to a comfortable chair.

"The fact is," said the chief, "the case is very simple, very simple indeed. And yet, it is very odd."

"Simple and odd," said Dupin.

"Why, yes," said the chief. "The truth is, we have all been quite puzzled because the case is so simple. But we can't figure it out."

"Perhaps it is too simple," said my friend.

"What nonsense you talk," replied the chief. He burst into laughter.

"Perhaps the mystery is a little *too* plain," said Dupin.

"Oh, good heavens! Who ever heard of such an idea?"

"Perhaps it is a little too obvious."

"Ha! ha! ha!" roared our visitor. "Oh, Dupin, you will be the death of me yet."

"What is the case about?" I asked.

"I will tell you," replied the chief. "But before I begin, let me caution you. The case is highly secret. I would probably lose my position if it became known that I discussed it with anyone."

"Begin," said I.

"Or not," said Dupin.

"Well then," said the chief, "I have received information. It comes from a highly placed person in the government. I have learned that something of the greatest importance has been purloined—yes, *stolen*—from an office in the royal palace."

We stared at the chief without saying a word.

"We know who stole it," the chief went on. "The man was seen taking it. It is also known that he has it still."

"And what is the name of the thief?" asked Dupin.

The chief lowered his voice. "The thief," he said, "is one of the most important and powerful ministers in the government. It is the Minister Darion."

"And what has been stolen?" I asked.

"The thing in question," said the chief, "is a letter. It is a letter which is immensely valuable because it could prove quite embarrassing to the government. It is therefore very important that we get it back as quickly as possible."

The chief paused. "And the responsibility for that has fallen to me."

"I can imagine," said Dupin, "no abler person for such a task."

"Thank you," said the chief of police.

"You are certain," said I, "that the minister still has the letter."

"Of that we are certain," said the chief. "My first move, therefore, was to search the minister's house. The problem lay in the need to search it without his finding this out. I had been warned of the danger which would result from giving him reason to suspect our plan."

"But," I said, "you are experienced in doing these things."

"Oh, yes," said he. "And therefore I was not very worried.

Besides, the habits of the minister gave me an advantage. He is often away from his home all night. He has just two servants, and they do not sleep in the house."

The chief took a deep breath before continuing. "I have keys, as you know, with which I can open any door in Paris. For many nights, I secretly searched the minister's house. My reputation is at stake. And, to mention a secret—the reward is enormous. So I did not stop searching until I had looked everywhere. I tell you, I looked through every corner and crack of that house. I looked every place where it is possible that letter could be hidden. And yet I found nothing!"

"But is it not possible," I asked, "that the minister has hidden the letter outside the house?"

"That is not possible," said Dupin. "It would be too dangerous. Besides, he is watched all the time."

"Then," I stated, "the letter must still be in the house. As for its being upon the person of the minister, is that out of the question?"

"Completely," said the chief. "Twice I arranged to have him robbed. He was carefully searched. Nothing was found."

"You might have saved yourself the trouble," said Dupin. "The minister is hardly a fool. He must have known that might happen."

"Suppose you tell us," I said, "exactly how you searched his home."

"Why," said the chief, "the fact is, we took our time. We searched *everywhere*. I went over the entire house, room by room. First we examined the furniture in each room. We opened every drawer. And I think you know, that to a well-trained police officer, such a thing as a 'secret' drawer is impossible. Next we looked at the chairs. The cushions we checked with the thin, metal needles you have seen me use.

"Then we removed the tops from the tables."

"Why?" I asked.

"The top of a table—or other piece of furniture—is sometimes removed by someone who wishes to conceal something. The person drills a hole into the leg. The thing is put into the hole. Then the top is put back on. The tops and bottoms of bedposts are often used this way."

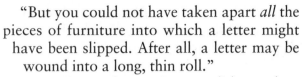

"But you could not have taken apart *all* the pieces of furniture into which a letter might have been slipped. After all, a letter may be wound into a long, thin roll."

"Certainly not. But we did even better. We brought a very powerful microscope. With it we carefully examined the wood on every piece of furniture in the house. Had there been any recent change, we would have spotted it at once. A few grains of dust would have looked as large as apples. Any change in the glue would immediately have been seen."

"I suppose you checked the mirrors. And the beds and the bedclothes, the curtains and carpets."

"Of course. And when we had finished examining everything in the house, then we looked at the house itself. We divided its entire surface into sections. We numbered each one so that none might be missed. Then we checked every square inch with our microscope."

"You went to a great deal of trouble," I said.

"I did. But the reward that was offered is huge."

"Did you look at the grounds around the house?"

"All the grounds are covered with brick. They gave us very little trouble. We looked at the moss between the bricks and found it untouched."

"You looked among the minister's papers, of course. And into the books in the library?"

"Certainly. We opened every book; we turned over every page in each volume. And we carefully checked the covers and backing."

"You explored the floors beneath the carpets?"

"Beyond doubt. We removed every carpet. Then we examined the boards with the microscope."

"And the paper on the walls?"

"Yes."

"You looked in the cellar?"

"We did."

"Then," I said, "you are mistaken. The letter is not in the house, as you think."

"I am afraid you are right," said the chief. He turned to Dupin. "And now, Dupin," he asked, "what do you suggest I do?"

"Search the house again."

"But that would serve no point," said the chief. "As sure as I am breathing, that letter is not in the house."

"I have no better advice to give you," said Dupin.

He looked closely at the chief. "You have an accurate description of the letter, of course."

"Oh, yes," said the chief. Here he took out a notebook. Slowly, he began to read a careful description of the letter. Soon afterward, he left. He seemed far sadder than I had ever seen the good gentleman before.

About a month later, the chief paid us another visit. I could hardly wait to speak to him. "Well," I asked, "what of the stolen letter?"

"As Dupin suggested, I searched the house again. But as I expected, nothing turned up."

"How much is the reward?" asked Dupin, slowly.

"Why, a very great deal—a great deal, indeed. I don't want to say exactly. But one thing I will tell you. I would gladly give a check for fifty thousand francs to anyone who could get me that letter."

"In that case," said Dupin, "you might as well write me a check for the amount you mentioned. And when you have signed it, I will hand you the letter."

I was astounded. The chief appeared thunderstruck. For several moments, he remained speechless and stared at my friend.

Finally, he recovered. Grabbing a pen, he wrote a check for fifty thousand francs and handed it to Dupin. Dupin looked at the check carefully. Then, unlocking a drawer, he pulled out a letter and gave it to the chief.

With a trembling hand, the chief unfolded the letter. He cast a quick glance at the words. Then rushing to the door, the chief dashed out.

When I had gotten over my surprise, I turned to Dupin. "Please explain," I said.

Now it's time for YOU to be the Reader as Detective.

How could Dupin know where the letter was hidden when the chief and his men were unable to find it? Where do you think Dupin might have looked? Think about the hints in the story before you read Part 2.

Be a Reading Detective

Read each of the following questions. Then write the letter of the correct answer to each question. Remember, the symbol next to each question identifies the *kind* of reading skill that particular question helps you to develop.

1. Dupin thought that the case was
   a. too hard.
   b. too simple.
   c. not very important
   d. not very interesting.

2. The letter was stolen from
   a. the royal palace.
   b. Gerrard's home.
   c. an office in the Paris police station.
   d. a minister's study.

3. Which happened last?
   a. Gerrard searched the minister's house.
   b. Dupin gave the chief a letter.
   c. Gerrard gave Dupin a check.
   d. Dupin said the case was too plain.

4. Dupin stated that "a letter may be wound into a long, thin roll." As used in this sentence, the word *wound* means
   a. broken.
   b. turned or twisted.
   c. a hurt or an injury.
   d. a clever hiding place.

5. What did the chief use when he searched the house?

   a. a powerful microscope
   b. metal needles
   c. both of the above
   d. none of the above

6. Which quotation from the story expresses an opinion?

   a. " 'I can imagine,' said Dupin, 'no abler person than you for such a task.' "
   b. " 'He has just two servants, and they do not sleep in the house.' "
   c. " 'First we examined the furniture in each room.' "
   d. " 'A few grains of dust would have looked as large as apples.' "

7. Gerrard arranged to have the minister

   a. beaten.
   b. robbed.
   c. given a reward.
   d. taken from his home.

8. You can infer that Dupin

   a. didn't know where the minister lived.
   b. didn't think he would find the letter.
   c went to the minister's house.
   d. questioned the minister about the letter.

9. The chief said, "We opened every book; we turned over every page in each volume." As used in this sentence, what is the meaning of the word *volume*?

   a. loudness
   b. space
   c. book
   d. collection

10. This selection tells mainly about

    a. the search for a stolen letter.

    b. the life of C. Auguste Dupin.

    c. the most powerful minister in the government.

    d. how police search houses.

Follow the Trail

Hints and Suggestions

In a mystery story, the author usually provides *hints* and *suggestions* that help the reader find the solution. As the Reader as Detective, you must learn to recognize these hints.

The correct answer to each of the following questions offers a hint or suggestion to finding the stolen letter.

11. According to Dupin, the mystery was

    a. impossible to solve.

    b. very uninteresting.

    c. possibly a little too plain.

    d. a wonderful challenge.

12. Dupin and the chief both agreed that

    a. the letter was not in the house.

    b. the letter was not on the person of the minister.

    c. the minister had the letter with him.

    d. the minister would make a mistake.

13. The chief and the police searched

    a. some of the rooms of the house.

    b. just the grounds around the house.

    c. every possible hiding place.

    d. the vehicles near the house.

14. Gerrard thought that the minister hid the letter

    a. in a secret spot.

    b. out in the open.

    c. in an office in the palace.

    d. in another house.

15. Dupin suggested that the chief

a. search the minister again.
b. search the house again.
c. forget about finding the letter.
d. search the palace.

Review your answers to the questions above. Keep them in mind as you read Part 2 of "The Purloined Letter."

Find Word Meanings

The five words listed below appear in "The Purloined Letter," Part 1. Study the words and their definitions. Use the page numbers to check how the words are used in the story. Then complete the following sentences by using each vocabulary word only *once*.

word	meaning	page
caution	warn	122
immensely	extremely great in size or quality	122
conceal	hide; keep secret	124
accurate	without errors; correct	125
astounded	greatly surprised	125

Mr. Gerrard, the chief of the Paris police, had a conversation with the famous detective C. Auguste Dupin. The chief said that he needed some advice about his newest case. He explained that it was his responsibility to find a letter someone had stolen—a purloined letter.

The chief was shocked and _____16_____ at what Dupin suggested. The detective said, "Let me warn and _____17_____ you. The answer to this mystery may be a little too clear and obvious."

Gerrard was _____18_____ amused at this suggestion. He could not believe that Dupin was correct, or _____19_____. Unable to _____20_____ his feelings, Gerrard burst into laughter.

Look at Language

Verbs

Like powerful adjectives, vivid verbs help to create descriptive language. As you may know, a **verb** is a word that shows action. Some examples of verbs are *stumbled*, *sneered*, *gasped*, and *blinked*. Notice how these vivid verbs help to create a picture or produce an effect.

Answer the following questions about verbs. Each question refers to the story.

21. " 'First we examined the furniture in each room. We opened every drawer.' " Which is most likely the meaning of the verb *examined* here?

    a. looked at carefully
    b. took apart
    c. tested
    d. slowly removed

22. "Then rushing to the door, the chief of police dashed out." Which of the following verbs could replace *dashed*?

    a. strolled
    b. walked
    c. hurried
    d. skipped

23. "Our conversation was interrupted by a loud knocking on the door. Dupin threw it open." Why do you think he *threw* it open?

    a. The door was heavy and he had to pull hard to open it.
    b. He was angry at the loud knocking.
    c. He was in a hurry because he thought the person knocking was in trouble.
    d. He was expecting good news and thought it had finally arrived.

24. What effect does the verb *grabbing* have on the sentence, "Grabbing a pen, he wrote a check for fifty thousand francs and handed it to Dupin"?

    a. It shows that Gerrard is very happy that the case is solved.

b. It shows that Gerrard is very eager to hear what Dupin has to say.

c. It shows that Gerrard has gone slightly mad with worry.

d. It shows that the two men trust each other quite deeply.

25. When the author writes that Gerrard *roared* with laughter, he is trying to show that Gerrard

a. thinks Dupin is a funny man.

b. thinks Dupin's idea is ridiculuous.

c. has a sense of humor.

d. has no respect for Dupin.

Review the Case

The following activities will help you review and reflect on what happened in "The Purloined Letter," Part 1.

1. **Discuss.** Do you have any ideas about where the letter was hidden? Could the police have missed it, or might it have been hidden somewhere else entirely? Discuss your ideas with your classmates.

2. **Write.** Suppose that Chief Gerrard wrote a police report describing his search for the hidden letter. What do you think the report would say? In a brief paragraph of four to five sentences, write Gerrard's report. (Note: Before you write your report, make a list of the items you wish to include. Then number them in the order in which you think they should appear. Use this outline as a guide in writing your report.)

3. **Technology Application.** In searches of crime scenes today, police look for a wide variety of evidence. Conduct research online and find at least five things police may search for and use as evidence in a case. Write a sentence or two explaining each one. Be sure to list what Web sites you used.

"We heard loud shots, and shouts coming from outside. The minister rushed to the window, threw it open, and looked out."

The Purloined Letter

PART 2

upin settled into a chair. "The police of Paris," said he, "are very able. They are hardworking and smart, and they know their business. So when the chief explained how they had searched the minister's house, I felt sure that they had done it very well—as far as they went."

"As far as they went?"

"Yes," said Dupin. "Their methods were the best of their kind, and carried out perfectly. Had the letter been within range of their search, those fellows would certainly have found it."

I laughed. But Dupin seemed quite serious in all that he said.

"Yes," said Dupin, "their methods were quite wrong for the man and the case."

"Wrong?" said I.

"You see," said Dupin, "the chief and his men consider only their *own* ideas of being clever. So in searching for anything hidden, they think of the ways in which *they* would have hidden it. Do you not see that the chief believes that *all* men would hide a letter in a hole drilled in a chair—or under a floorboard, or in some out-of-the-way place? And had the letter been hidden in that kind of secret spot, they would surely have found it."

"But the minister is a man of great intelligence. I felt sure he was aware of the methods to be used against him. He must have known that he himself would be robbed. He must have known that his home would be searched."

Dupin paused for a moment. "Yes," said he, "the chief was delighted that the minister so often stayed away from home all night. But I immediately saw this as a trick by the minister. He purposely stayed away—to give the police plenty of time to carefully search the house. Thus they could convince themselves that the letter was not there."

"But what happened to the letter?"

"The minister," said Dupin, "must have known how foolish it would be to hide it in any of the usual hiding spots. He must have known how every out-of-the-way space would be searched. I realized that he would be forced to do something *simple*. Remember how the chief laughed when I first suggested that perhaps this mystery troubled him so much because it was so obvious."

"I remember it well. How loudly he laughed."

A smile crossed Dupin's face. He continued to smile.

"But *what of* the letter?" I demanded.

Now it's time for YOU to be the Reader as Detective.

 Where do you think the minister "hid" the letter? Dupin's words should help you decide where to look. Read on to see if you are right!

"The chief never once," Dupin went on, "thought it probable or possible that the minister had deposited the letter beneath the nose of the whole world—as the best way of preventing the world from seeing it. Yes, the more I thought about it, the more convinced I became that to hide the letter, the minister had decided on the excellent plan of not hiding it at all.

"With this idea in mind, I put on a pair of green glasses. Then I called at the minister's home. Once in his study, I complained to him of my weak eyes because of which, I explained, I wore the glasses. Under their cover, I carefully looked around. All the while, I made believe I was very interested in what the minister was saying.

"I paid keen attention to a large desk. On it were some letters, papers, a musical instrument, and a few books. I looked at them carefully and long. But I saw nothing to make me suspicious. I continued to look around the room. Finally, my eyes stopped on an old cardboard letter holder. It was hanging from a blue ribbon attached to a nail over the fireplace.

"The holder had three compartments. In them were five or six cards and a letter. The letter was soiled and crumpled, and was torn nearly in half across the middle. It looked as though someone had decided to tear it up and had then changed his mind. The letter was addressed to the minister in small, clear handwriting. It seemed to have been thrown carelessly into one of the compartments of the rack.

"As soon as I saw this letter, I was sure it was the very one for which I was searching. It is true that it appeared quite different from the letter which the chief had described to us. In that one, the handwriting was large, and the letter was addressed to a member of the government. Here the handwriting was small, and the letter was addressed to the minister. Still, this letter was dirty and torn, unusual for a minister so tidy and neat. And that it should be there, in the full view of every visitor—that made me suspicious.

"I stayed as long as possible. All the while, I kept talking about a subject that I knew the minister found fascinating. But I kept staring at the letter. I set my mind to remembering exactly how it looked and its place in the rack. Finally, I made a discovery that convinced me I was right!"

"What was that?" I asked eagerly.

"In looking at the edges of the paper, I noticed them to be more broken than seemed necessary. It was as though the letter had been folded, and then folded again in the *opposite* direction. It was clear to me that the letter had been turned, as a glove, inside out, and had been addressed again. I said goodbye to the minister and went out. But I made sure to leave my cigarette case on the table.

"The next morning I returned for the cigarette case. While the minister and I were talking, we heard loud shots, and shouts coming from outside. The minister rushed to the window, threw it open, and looked out. At that moment, I stepped to the letter holder. I quickly took the letter and put it into my pocket. I replaced it with another letter which looked exactly like the first.

"The problem outside had been caused by a man with a gun. He had been firing it at a crowd. However, it seems that he was only firing blanks, so they called the fellow a madman and let him go on his way. A few moments later, I left the minister's house. The 'madman,' of course, was a man I had hired."

"Excellent!" I said. "Excellent! But why did you replace the letter with another that looked just like it? Wouldn't it have been better, at the first visit, to have grabbed the letter and run?"

"The minister," said Dupin, "is an exceedingly dangerous man. His house is not without guards. Had I made the wild attempt you suggest, I might never have left him alive. The good people of Paris would have heard of me no more."

Dupin began to laugh. "I confess," he said, "I would very much like to be there when he opens the letter which I left in the letter rack."

"Why? Did you write anything special in it?"

"It did not seem right to leave the inside of the letter blank. So I just wrote in these words:

> *Your little plan was quite well done.*
> *But my plan was a better one.*"

Be a Reading Detective

Read each of the following questions. Then write the letter of the correct answer to each question. Remember, the symbol next to each question identifies the *kind* of reading skill that particular question helps you to develop.

1. Before Dupin went to the minister's house, he put on
   a. green gloves.
   b. green glasses.
   c. a dark suit.
   d. a heavy coat.

2. Where did the minister "hide" the letter?

a. under a floorboard
b. in a hole drilled in a chair
c. in a cardboard letter holder
d. in a pile on his desk

3. Which happened last?

a. The minister rushed to the window and threw it open.
b. Dupin complained about his weak eyes.
c. Dupin quickly took the letter and put it his pocket.
d. The men heard shots from outside.

4. The man with the gun

a. was crazy.
b. had been hired by Dupin.
c. was one of the minister's guards.
d. was taken to jail.

5. You can infer that

a. the police noticed the letter but did not examine it.
b. the minister placed the letter where no one could see it.
c. the minister was foolish for putting the letter where the chief could see it.
d. the minister made copies of the letter.

6. The letter in the letter holder was

a. tidy and neat.
b. dirty and torn.
c. addressed to a member of the government.
d. folded in half.

7. Which quotation expresses an opinion?

a. " 'The next morning I returned for the cigarette case.' "
b. " 'Had I made the wild attempt you suggest, I might never have left him alive.' "

c. " 'I paid keen attention to a large desk.' "
d. " 'But I immediately saw this as a trick by the minister.' "

8. Dupin suggested that the minister "deposited the letter beneath the nose of the whole world." What is the meaning of the word *deposited*?

a. mailed
b. placed
c. wrote
d. copied

9. How do you think the minister felt when he read the poem?

a. amused
b. pleasantly surprised
c. furious
d. confused

10. Which of the following BEST tells the main idea of this selection?

a. The chief is unable to find the letter.
b. Dupin outwits the minister.
c. The minister knew that his home would be searched.
d. Dupin hires a madman to help him.

Follow the Trail

Missing Pieces

Often, good detective work means "putting the pieces together" in a case. Sometimes, however, one or more of the pieces may be missing. Then the detective must look closely at the evidence and use his or her reason to figure out what is missing.

The reader as detective also must be able to figure out what's missing. First review the facts found in a story. Then use your reason to supply scenes and events that do not actually appear in the selection. The following questions will help you develop this skill.

11. After he left the minister's house, Dupin must have

 a. called Chief Gerrard for help.
 b. wondered where the letter was hidden.
 c. made a letter like the one he had seen.
 d. taken the letter to the chief.

12. Although the scene does not appear in the story, we can be sure that Dupin discussed with another man

 a. how to overpower the minister's guards.
 b. where and when to fire a gun.
 c. when to attack the minister.
 d. where to find the letter.

13. Before Gerrard searched the house, the minister

 a. hid the letter in the basement.
 b. turned the letter inside out and addressed it again.
 c. put an extra lock on the door.
 d. hid the letter in his jacket.

14. Dupin made two visits to the minister's house. Between the visits, Dupin

 a. wrote a brief poem.
 b. called the police.
 c. hired a guard to protect him.
 d. visited a madhouse.

15. What did Dupin do with the letter he took from the rack?

 a. He brought it to the police station.
 b. He returned it to an official in the government.
 c. He took it back to his apartment.
 d. He gave it to a palace guard.

Find Word Meanings

The five words listed on the next page appear in "The Purloined Letter," Part 2. Study the words and their definitions. Use the page numbers to check how the words are used in the story. Then complete the following sentences by using each vocabulary word only *once*.

word	meaning	page
intelligence	ability to learn and know	132
probable	likely to happen; likely to be true	133
keen	sharp	133
fascinating	of very great interest	134
exceedingly	very; greatly	135

Edgar Allan Poe was an _____16_____ important American author. Poe wrote short stories and poems. He was also a well-known literary critic.

Poe's life and works were unusually interesting and _____17_____. Because of this, it is likely, or _____18_____, that more books have been written about Poe than about any other American writer.

Poe's character C. Auguste Dupin appears in three of Poe's short stories. Like Sherlock Holmes, Dupin was a careful, _____19_____ observer. Like Holmes, Dupin used his _____20_____ to solve crimes.

Look at Language

Adverbs

Adverbs are used to describe verbs, adjectives, or other adverbs. That means that they describe how, when, or to what degree an action is performed. Sometimes adverbs are easy to identify because they frequently end in *ly*. Adverbs can describe when an action takes place with words like *often* or *later*. They can also describe degrees of something such as *very* cold or *less* friendly.

Answer the following questions about adverbs that appear in Part 2 of "The Purloined Letter."

21. Which phrase from the story contains an adverb?
   a. very able
   b. their kind
   c. being clever
   d. secret spot

22. Which adverb describes the way Dupin took the letter on page 135?

    a. rushed
    b. replaced
    c. quickly
    d. exactly

23. Which of these words from the story is *not* an adverb?

    a. finally
    b. carelessly
    c. quite
    d. anything

24. Which sentence from the story contains an adverb?

    a. " 'I continued to look around the room.' "
    b. " 'How loudly he laughed.' "
    c. " 'But I kept staring at the letter.' "
    d. "Dupin began to laugh."

25. Below are four groups of words. Identify the group that contains *only* adverbs.

    a. certainly, surely, often
    b. only, purposely, troubled
    c. immediately, continued, seeing
    d. nearly, pair, complained

Review the Case

The following activities will help you review and reflect on what happened in "The Purloined Letter," Part 2.

1. Discuss. At what point in the story was Dupin sure that he had found the letter for which he was searching?

2. Write. What could possibly have been written in the letter to make it so dangerous? Imagine the story took place today, in the United States. Write a version of the letter, and be sure to include material (that you make up, of course) that would be as valuable and dangerous as that in the purloined letter of the story.

3. Technology Application. What if the story were written in modern times, and the message was a text message instead of a letter? Write a short, text message version of the letter you wrote for number 2 above. Which two people might send and receive such a text message?

Bobby was experiencing a burning sensation in his feet, numbness in his hands, a flushed face, and intense sweating.

Joann Curley: Caught by a Hair

by Richard Saferstein

A vibrant young woman named Joann Curley rushed to the Wilkes-Barre (Pennsylvania) General Hospital—her husband, Bobby, was having an attack and required immediate medical attention. Bobby was experiencing a burning sensation in his feet, numbness in his hands, a flushed face, and intense sweating. He was diagnosed with Guillain-Barré syndrome, an acute inflammation of the nervous system that accounted for all of Bobby's symptoms. After being discharged, Bobby experienced another bout of debilitating pain and numbness. He was admitted to another hospital, the larger and more capable Hershey Medical Center in Hershey, Pennsylvania. There doctors observed extreme alopecia, or hair loss. Test results of Bobby's urine showed high levels of the heavy metal thallium in his body. Thallium, a rare and highly toxic metal that was used decades ago in substances such as rat poison and to treat ringworm and gout, was found in sufficient quantities to cause Bobby's sickness. The use of thallium was banned in the United States in 1984. Now, at least, Bobby could be treated. However, before Bobby's doctor could treat him for thallium poisoning, he experienced cardiac arrest and slipped into a coma. Joann Curley made the difficult decision to remove her husband of thirteen months from life support equipment. He died shortly thereafter.

Now it's time for YOU to be the Reader as Detective.

The title of the story is "Joann Curley: Caught by a Hair." After reading the first section of the article, do you think this is a simple case of accidental poisoning? What will the rest of the article be about?

Read on to find out.

Bobby Curley was an electrician and, for five months before his death, he worked in the chemistry department at nearby Wilkes University. Authorities suspected that Bobby had been accidentally exposed to thallium there among old chemicals and laboratory equipment. The laboratory was searched and several old bottles of powdered thallium salts were discovered in a storage closet. After testing the air and surfaces, these were eliminated as possible sources for exposure. This finding was supported by the discovery that none of Bobby's co-workers had any thallium in their systems. The next most logical route of exposure was in the home; thus, the Curley kitchen was sampled. Of the hundreds of items tested, three thermoses were found to contain traces of thallium.

Investigators also learned that Bobby had changed his life insurance to list his wife, Joann, as the beneficiary of his $300,000 policy. Based on this information, police consulted a forensic toxicologist in an effort to glean as much from the physical evidence in Bobby Curley's body as possible. The toxicologist conducted segmental analysis of Bobby's hair, an analytical method based on the predictable rate of hair growth on the human scalp: an average of 1 centimeter per month. Bobby had approximately 5 inches (12.5 centimeters) of hair, which represents almost twelve months of hair growth. Each section tested represented a specific period of time in Bobby's final year of his life.

The hair analysis proved that Bobby Curley was poisoned with thallium long before he began working at Wilkes University. The first few doses were small, which probably barely made him sick at the time. Gradually, over a year or more, Bobby was receiving more doses of thallium until he finally succumbed to a massive dose three or four days before his death. After careful scrutiny of the time line, investigators concluded that only Joann Curley had

Poisons can be anywhere, so you should be aware of their location, whether camping out in the woods, or caring for your younger brothers and sisters at home. Here are some helpful suggestions.

Why do babysitters or teens need to know about poison?

Caring for children is a great job, but keeping children safe is a serious and important part of babysitting.

Poisoning is one of the most common childhood injuries.

Most of the time poisoning happens right at home. Children who are between the ages of eight months and six years old are the most likely to be poisoned.

Poisons can look like things that are good to eat and drink. They can come in many colors and forms including solids, liquids, sprays or gases. Young children are curious. They like to put things in their mouths, especially if they look colorful or smell nice. It's a good idea to have emergency information handy when you're babysitting.

What are some common poisons?

Poisonous products that may be found in and around the home:

■ medicines
■ iron pills
■ cleaning products
■ laundry products
■ nail polish and remover
■ batteries
■ bug and weed killers
■ cigarettes
■ alcohol
■ mouthwash
■ plants (indoor and outdoor)
■ lighter fluids

How can children be kept safe from poison?

Follow these safety tips:

■ Keep children where you can see them at all times, even when you go to answer the door or telephone. Never leave young children alone, not even for just a minute!

■ All medicines and household cleaning products should be stored in locked cabinets, out of the reach

access to Bobby during each of these intervals. She also had a motive, in the amount of $300,000.

Presented with the time line and the solid toxicological evidence against her, Joann Curley pleaded guilty to murder. As part of her plea agreement, she provided a forty-page written confession of how she haphazardly dosed Bobby with some rat poison she found in her basement. She admitted that she murdered him for the money she would receive from Bobby's life insurance policy.

and sight of children. Do not leave poisons on a counter or in an unlocked cabinet.

■ Never carry something that can be poisonous, such as a medicine, in a purse where children may find it.

■ Safety latches on drawers or cabinets, and child-resistant caps on bottles, are helpful in keeping poisons out of the hands of children. But remember, they are not "child-proof" and do not substitute for your careful and constant supervision.

Remember the BEFORE, WHILE, and AFTER Rule

BEFORE using a cleaning product, read the instructions on the bottle.

WHILE using a cleaning product, never leave it alone. A child may find it.

AFTER using a product, put it back in a locked cabinet. Make sure the container is closed tightly.

If you are asked to give medicine to a child, follow the instructions on the bottle. After using the medicine, return the bottle to a safe storage place right away. Never leave a child alone with the medicine.

What information about each child should you have?

Before parents leave you in charge of a child, make sure they write down some basic information such as:

■ each child's age and weight
■ any allergies or medical conditions
■ their doctor's name and telephone number
■ how the parents can be reached in an emergency

Get Help

If you think someone has been poisoned, call **1-800-222-1222** right away. Do not wait for the child to look or feel sick. The poison center will tell you what to do to help the child. Make sure you know the poison center's telephone number. Keep a card or sticker with the poison center's telephone number, carry it with you on your babysitting jobs and save the number in your cell phone.

For more poison prevention and first aid information call **1-800-222-1222**.

Be a Reading Detective

Read each of the following questions. Then write the letter of the correct answer to each question. Remember, the symbol next to each question identifies the *kind* of reading skill that particular question helps you to develop.

1. This selection is mainly about
   a. how the police figured out that Joann Curley killed her husband.
   b. the steps Joann Curley took to kill her husband.
   c. Joann Curley's reasons for killing her husband.
   d. what kind of man Bobby Curley had been.

2. Which is another word for *sensation* in the first paragraph?
   a. disturbance
   b. pain
   c. feeling
   d. itching

3. The most important idea in the second paragraph is that
   a. Bobby Curley had received many doses of thallium over time.
   b. investigators performed analysis on Bobby Curley's hair.
   c. one large dose of thallium killed Bobby Curley.
   d. Joann Curley stood to gain a lot of money from her husband's death.

4. How did Bobby Curley die?
   a. He experienced a massive heart attack.
   b. His nervous system became inflamed.
   c. His wife removed him from life support.
   d. He was in a coma for too long.

5. What does the author mean by, "She also had a motive, in the amount of $300,000," in the fourth paragraph?

   a. Joann Curley could run away now that her husband was gone.
   b. Joann Curley had taken out a separate life insurance policy.
   c. Joann Curley increased the amount of her husband's life insurance.
   d. Joann Curley would receive money from Bobby Curley's life insurance.

6. Using Bobby Curley's hair, investigators could trace physical evidence going back about

   a. three months.
   b. one year.
   c. 10 weeks.
   d. 72 days.

7. Which of the following is a fact in the case?

   a. Joann Curley loved her husband.
   b. Joann Curley was a vibrant woman.
   c. Bobby Curley died with low levels of thallium in his system.
   d. Bobby Curley was poisoned with thallium before he began working at Wilkes University.

8. How did investigators know the thallium in the lab was not the source of Bobby Curley's poisoning?

   a. The thallium in the lab was not the kind that poisons.
   b. the thallium in the lab was too old to do any damage.
   c. Bobby Curley didn't actually ingest the thallium in the lab.
   d. The levels of thallium in the lab were not high enough.

9. On the time line the police presented, which might have come first?

   a. Bobby Curley married Joann Curley.
   b. Joann Curley poisoned her husband with thallium.
   c. Bobby Curley worked in a university lab.
   d. Police analyzed samples of Bobby Curley's hair.

10. Based on the information in the selection, what is most likely the meaning of the word *scrutiny* in the fourth paragraph?

    a. close positioning
    b. careful examination
    c. easy access
    d. legal reasoning

Follow the Trail

Author's Purpose

Authors write for different reasons. One reason is to **entertain** the reader. For example, an author might write a mystery story to keep you at the edge of your seat, or a funny story to make you laugh. Another reason authors write is to **inform** the reader about something. For example, a textbook author might want to teach you about U.S. history. A third reason authors write is to **persuade** the reader. For example, a newspaper or magazine article might convince you to vote for someone or something.

The following questions will give you practice identifying author's purpose in "Joann Curley: Caught by a Hair."

11. The purpose of this article is mostly to

    a. inform the reader about thallium poisoning in the U.S.
    b. persuade the reader to become a forensic toxicologist.
    c. entertain the reader with a story about a murder investigation.
    d. share a personal experience with the reader.

12. "The use of thallium was banned in the United States in 1984."

Why might the author have included this detail?

a. to prove that doctors were wrong about thallium being in Bobby's body
b. to reveal that Joann Curley was guilty of the crime
c. to show that Bobby's death might be the result of foul play
d. to show that the thallium ban has some medicinal purposes

13. What is the purpose of the sidebar?

a. to convince parents that they shouldn't trust babysitters
b. to inform people about poison safety and prevention
c. to convince parents to buy safer cleaning supplies
d. to inform people about how a poison center works

14. Why did the sidebar author include the statement, "Poisoning is one of the most common childhood injuries"?

a. to stress that poisoning can indeed happen, so you need to be prepared
b. to show that poisoning is common and is therefore nothing to worry about
c. to explain why a local poison control center might be too busy for calls
d. to highlight the problems with poor parenting in America

15. Why did the sidebar author include the list of common poisons?

a. to show that poisons are rare and don't exist in most homes
b. to show that poisons exist in things you actually use
c. to convince parents to stop using such harmful chemicals
d. to show that most poisons are found in medicine cabinets.

Find Word Meanings

The five words listed below appear in "Joann Curley: Caught by a Hair." Study the words and their definitions. Use the page numbers to check how the words are used in the story. Then complete the following sentences by using each vocabulary word only *once*.

word	meaning	page
vibrant	bright, lively, and energetic	142
inflammation	swelling; irritation	142
debilitating	making something or someone unable to function properly	142
sufficient	enough; able to satisfy a need	143
beneficiary	the recipient of something good, somebody or something that gets money	143

At first, doctors couldn't determine the cause of the swelling or _____16_____ that Bobby Curley was experiencing and that was causing _____17_____ pain. However, they soon discovered it was thallium poisoning. At that point, investigators and toxicologists joined the case and gathered _____18_____ evidence to prove that Joann Curley had poisoned her husband. Joann eventually pleaded guilty. On the outside, she may have seemed like a happy, _____19_____ woman, but on the inside, she was a disturbed person who would do anything to be the _____20_____ of her husband's life insurance.

Look at Language

Verb-Adverb Pairs

As you've learned, **verbs** lend strong action to stories and **adverbs** can help to describe events in vivid detail. Look back at the "Look at Language" sections on verbs (page 130) and adverbs (page 139) to refresh your memory. Then answer these questions about "Joann Curley: Caught by a Hair."

21. Which verb does the adverb *barely* describe in the sentence below?

"The first few doses were small, which probably barely made him sick at the time."

a. were
b. sick
c. probably
d. made

22. Which verb does the adverb *shortly* modify in the sentence below?

"Joann Curley made the difficult decision to remove her husband of thirteen months from life support equipment. He died shortly thereafter."

a. He
b. died
c. decision
d. made

23. Identify the verb-adverb pair in the following sentence:

"Gradually, over a year or more, Bobby was receiving more doses of thallium until he finally succumbed to a massive dose three or four days before his death."

a. "was receiving"
b. "more doses"
c. "massive dose"
d. "finally succumbed"

24. Identify the verb-adverb pair in the following sentence:

"Authorities suspected that Bobby had been accidentally exposed to thallium there among old chemicals and laboratory equipment."

a. "Authorities suspected"
b. "old chemicals"
c. "accidentally exposed"
d. "laboratory equipment"

25. Read the following sentence from the article.

"As part of her plea agreement, she provided a forty-page written confession of how she haphazardly dosed Bobby with some rat poison she found in her basement."

The phrase "haphazardly dosed" means

a. long document.
b. quickly killed.
c. rodent killer.
d. randomly drugged.

Review the Case

The following activities will help you review and reflect on what happened in "Joann Curley: Caught by a Hair."

1. Discuss. What safety measures could you take to ensure that a child is safe from accidental poisoning? Discuss these measures with your classmates.

2. Write. Imagine that the Joann Curley story was an episode of a TV crime show. Write a screenplay for that episode. First, list what actors you would have play each role (narrator, Joann, Bobby, doctors, investigators). Then rewrite the story as a script, using narration and dialogue.

3. Technology Application. There are many kinds of crime scene investigators, such as forensic toxicologists, forensic odontologists, and forensic pathologists. Choose one of these types of forensic scientists. Research what kind of training they have and what is involved in their work. Write a brief paragraph about your findings.

They stood looking at the door and saw it tremble from her beating and throwing herself against it. They heard her muffled cries.

All Summer in a Day

by Ray Bradbury

Now it's time for YOU to be the Reader as Detective.

This story has an interesting title—"All Summer in a Day." What do you think it means? How could an entire season be contained in one day? Before you read the story, try to predict what it might be about.

EADY?"

"Ready."

"Now?"

"Soon."

"Do the scientists really know? Will it happen today, will it?"

"Look, look; see for yourself!"

The children pressed to each other like so many roses, so many weeds, intermixed, peering out for a look at the hidden sun.

It rained.

It had been raining for seven years; thousands upon thousands of days compounded and filled from one end to the other with rain, with the drum and gush of water, with the sweet crystal fall of

showers and the concussion of storms so heavy they were tidal waves come over the islands. A thousand forests had been crushed under the rain and grown up a thousand times to be crushed again. And this was the way life was forever on the planet Venus, and this was the schoolroom of the children of the rocket men and women who had come to a raining world to set up civilization and live out their lives.

"It's stopping, it's stopping!"

"Yes, yes!"

Margot stood apart from them, from these children who could never remember a time when there wasn't rain and rain and rain. They were all nine years old, and if there had been a day, seven years ago, when the sun came out for an hour and showed its face to the stunned world, they could not recall. Sometimes, at night, she heard them stir, in remembrance, and she knew they were dreaming and remembering gold or a yellow crayon or a coin large enough to buy the world with. She knew they thought they remembered a warmness, like a blushing in the face, in the body, in the arms and legs and trembling hands. But then they always awoke to the tatting drum, the endless shaking down of clear bead necklaces upon the roof, the walk, the gardens, the forests, and their dreams were gone.

All day yesterday they had read in class about the sun. About how like a lemon it was, and how hot. And they had written small stories or essays or poems about it:

> *I think the sun is a flower,*
>
> *That blooms for just one hour.*

That was Margot's poem, read in a quiet voice in the still classroom while the rain was falling outside.

"Aw, you didn't write that!" protested one of the boys.

"I did," said Margot. "*I did.*"

"William!" said the teacher.

But that was yesterday. Now the rain was slackening, and the children were crushed in the great thick windows.

"Where's teacher?"

"She'll be back."

"She'd better hurry, we'll miss it!"

They turned on themselves, like a feverish wheel, all tumbling spokes.

Margot stood alone. She was a very frail girl who looked as if she had been lost in the rain for years and the rain had washed out the blue from her eyes and the red from her mouth and the yellow from her hair. She was an old photograph dusted from an album, whitened away, and if she spoke at all her voice would be a ghost. Now she stood, separate, staring at the rain and the loud wet world beyond the huge glass.

"What're *you* looking at?" said William.

Margot said nothing.

"Speak when you're spoken to." He gave her a shove. But she did not move; rather she let herself be moved only by him and nothing else.

They edged away from her, they would not look at her. She felt them go away. And this was because she would play no games with them in the echoing tunnels of the underground city. If they tagged her and ran, she stood blinking after them and did not follow. When the class sang songs about happiness and life and games her lips barely moved. Only when they sang about the sun and the summer did her lips move as she watched the drenched windows.

And then, of course, the biggest crime of all was that she had come here only five years ago from Earth, and she remembered the sun and the way the sun was and the sky was when she was four in Ohio. And they, they had been on Venus all their lives, and they had been only two years old when last the sun came out and had long since forgotten the color and heat of it and the way it really was. But Margot remembered.

"It's like a penny," she said once, eyes closed.

"No it's not!" the children cried.

"It's like a fire," she said, "in the stove."

"You're lying, you don't remember!" cried the children.

But she remembered and stood quietly apart from all of them and watched the patterning windows. And once, a month ago, she had refused to shower in the school shower rooms, had clutched her hands to her ears and over her head, screaming the water mustn't touch her head. So after that, dimly, she sensed it, she was different and they knew her difference and kept away.

There was talk that her father and mother were taking her back to Earth next year; it seemed vital to her that they do so, though it would mean the loss of thousands of dollars to her family. And so, the children hated her for all these reasons of big and little consequence. They hated her pale snow face, her waiting silence, her thinness, and her possible future.

"Get away!" The boy gave her another push. "What're you waiting for?"

Then, for the first time, she turned and looked at him. And what she was waiting for was in her eyes.

"Well, don't wait around here!" cried the boy savagely. "You won't see nothing!"

Her lips moved.

"Nothing!" he cried. "It was all a joke, wasn't it?" He turned to the other children. "Nothing's happening today. *Is* it?"

They all blinked at him and then, understanding, laughed and shook their heads. "Nothing, nothing!"

"Oh, but," Margot whispered, her eyes helpless. "But this is the day, the scientists predict, they say, they *know*, the sun . . ."

"All a joke!" said the boy, and seized her roughly. "Hey, everyone, let's put her in a closet before teacher comes!"

"No," said Margot, falling back.

They surged about her, caught her up and bore her, protesting, and then pleading, and then crying, back into a tunnel, a room, a closet, where they slammed and locked the door. They stood looking at the door and saw it tremble from her beating and throwing herself against it. They heard her muffled cries. Then, smiling, they turned and went out and back down the tunnel, just as the teacher arrived.

"Ready, children?" She glanced at her watch.

"Yes!" said everyone.

"Are we all here?"

"Yes!"

The rain slackened still more.

They crowded to the huge door.

The rain stopped.

It was as if, in the midst of a film concerning an avalanche, a tornado, a hurricane, a volcanic eruption, something had, first, gone wrong with the sound apparatus, thus muffling and finally cutting off all noise, all of the blasts and repercussions and thunders, and then, second, ripped the film from the projector and inserted in its place a peaceful tropical slide which did not move or tremor. The world ground to a standstill. The silence was so immense and unbelievable that you felt your ears had been stuffed or you had lost your hearing altogether. The children put their

hands to their ears. They stood apart. The door slid back and the smell of the silent, waiting world came in to them.

The sun came out.

It was the color of flaming bronze and it was very large. And the sky around it was a blazing blue tile color. And the jungle burned with sunlight as the children, released from their spell, rushed out, yelling, into the springtime.

"Now, don't go too far," called the teacher after them. "You've only two hours, you know. You wouldn't want to get caught out!"

But they were running and turning their faces up to the sky and feeling the sun on their cheeks like a warm iron; they were taking off their jackets and letting the sun burn their arms.

"Oh, it's better than the sun lamps, isn't it?"

"Much, much better!"

They stopped running and stood in the great jungle that covered Venus, that grew and never stopped growing, tumultuously, even as you watched it. It was a nest of octopi, clustering up great arms of fleshlike weed, wavering, flowering in this brief spring. It was the color of rubber and ash, this jungle, from the many years without sun. It was the color of stones and white cheeses and ink, and it was the color of the moon.

The children lay out, laughing, on the jungle mattress, and heard it sigh and squeak under them, resilient and alive. They ran among the trees, they slipped and fell, they pushed each other, they played hide-and-seek and tag, but most of all they squinted at the sun until tears ran down their faces, they put their hands up to that yellowness and that amazing blueness and they breathed of the fresh, fresh air and listened and listened to the silence which suspended them in a blessed sea of no sound and no motion. They looked at everything and savored everything. Then, wildly, like animals escaped from their caves, they ran and ran in shouting circles. They ran for an hour and did not stop running.

And then—

In the midst of their running one of the girls wailed.

Everyone stopped.

The girl, standing in the open, held out her hand.

"Oh, look, look," she said, trembling.

They came slowly to look at her opened palm.

In the center of it, cupped and huge, was a single raindrop.

She began to cry, looking at it.

They glanced quietly at the sky.

"Oh. Oh."

A few cold drops fell on their noses and their cheeks and their mouths. The sun faded behind a stir of mist. A wind blew cool around them. They turned and started to walk back toward the underground house, their hands at their sides, their smiles vanishing away.

A boom of thunder startled them and like leaves before a new hurricane, they tumbled upon each other and ran. Lightning struck ten miles away, five miles away, a mile, a half mile. The sky darkened into midnight in a flash.

They stood in the doorway of the underground for a moment until it was raining hard. Then they closed the door and heard the gigantic sound of the rain falling in tons and avalanches, everywhere and forever.

"Will it be seven more years?"

"Yes. Seven."

Then one of them gave a little cry.

"Margot!"

"What?"

"She's still in the closet where we locked her."

"Margot."

They stood as if someone had driven them, like so many stakes, into the floor. They looked at each other and then looked away. They glanced out at the world that was raining now and raining and raining steadily. They could not meet each other's glances. Their faces were solemn and pale. They looked at their hands and feet, their faces down.

"Margot."

One of the girls said, "Well . . . ?"

No one moved.

"Go on," whispered the girl.

They walked slowly down the hall in the sound of cold rain. They turned through the doorway to the room in the sound of the storm and thunder, lightning on their faces, blue and terrible. They walked over the closet door slowly and stood by it.

Behind the closet door was only silence.

They unlocked the door, even more slowly, and let Margot out.

Be a Reading Detective

Read each of the following questions. Then write the letter of the correct answer to each question. Remember, the symbol next to each question identifies the *kind* of reading skill that particular question helps you to develop.

1. Margot has been on Venus for just five years, but the other children have been there

    a. for the last seven years.

    b. for at least ten years.

    c. since they were two years old.

    d. since they were born.

2. "She was a very frail girl who looked as if she had been lost in the rain for years and the rain had washed out the blue from her eyes and the red from her mouth and the yellow from her hair." What is most likely the meaning of the word *frail*?

   a. quiet
   b. weak
   c. shy
   d. boring

3. Which is an opinion about Margot?

   a. She wrote a poem about the sun.
   b. She lived on Earth until she was four years old.
   c. She doesn't stand up for herself enough.
   d. She was locked in the closet.

4. Why does Margot change from her usual quiet self when the children lock her in the closet on page 156?

   a. Margot is fighting back because she's tired of being bullied.
   b. Margot is hoping the teacher will hear her from inside the closet.
   c. Margot is desperate to see the one thing that could make her happy.
   d. Margot is scared she will suffocate in the closet.

5. What happened after the children put Margot in the closet?

   a. They teased her.
   b. The teacher came.
   c. Margot was quiet.
   d. Margot sang about the sun.

6. Why does the girl cry when she first feels the raindrop?

   a. She's afraid of the lightning that might follow.

b. She feels bad Margot is in the closet.
c. She doesn't want to get her hair wet.
d. She doesn't want her fun in the sun to end.

7. The main idea of the paragraph that begins "The children lay out" (page 158) is that

a. the sun finally came out.
b. the jungle is growing everywhere.
c. the children enjoyed the sun.
d. the children stared at the sun.

8. Which of the following is *not* true in the story?

a. Margot didn't write the poem she read in class.
b. The children eventually let Margot out of the closet.
c. It rains for seven years at a time on Venus.
d. Margot remembers what the sun was like.

9. The main idea the author is trying to convey at the end of the story (page 159) is that

a. the children feel guilty once they realize what they took from Margot.
b. the children are horribly cruel for what they did to Margot.
c. the teacher is angry when she realizes that Margot was trapped.
d. Margot should have fought harder to free herself from the closet.

10. What will most likely happen to Margot after the end of the story?

a. She will die of a broken heart.
b. Her parents will take her back to Earth.
c. She will tell the teacher what the children did.
d. She will refuse to take a shower.

Follow the Trail

Figurative Language

As you learned, **figurative language** uses words in creative, imaginative ways, to create images and feelings for readers as they journey through a story. Two kinds of figurative language are **similes** and **metaphors**. A simile compares two unlike things using the word *like* or *as* (for example, "I swim like a fish"). A metaphor is a direct comparison of two unlike things that does not use *like* or *as* (for example, "I am a fish in the ocean").

"All Summer in a Day" is filled with similes and metaphors. Figuring out the meanings of these expressions will give you a better understanding of the events and characters in the story. The following questions will help you practice this skill.

11. Remember that a simile compares two things. Which words form the simile in the sentence below?

   "The children pressed to each other like so many roses, so many weeds, intermixed, peering out for a look at the hidden sun."
   a. "The children pressed to each other"
   b. "like so many roses, so many weeds"
   c. "intermixed, peering out"
   d. "a look at the hidden sun"

12. Which sentence from the story does *not* contain a simile?
   a. "It's like a penny."
   b. "It's like a fire."
   c. "They were . . . feeling the sun on their cheeks like a warm iron."
   d. "It was the color of flaming bronze."

13. "They turned on themselves, like a feverish wheel, all tumbling spokes."

   The simile in this sentence shows you that the children were
   a. patiently waiting for the sun.
   b. depressed about the rain.
   c. practically falling over each other with excitement.
   d. feeling sick and feverish because of the rain.

14. "She was an old photograph dusted from an album, whitened away, and if she spoke at all her voice would be a ghost."

The metaphor comparing Margot to an old photograph shows you that she

a. was weak and depressed, missing her former life.
b. had a pretty face, like that of actresses in old photographs.
c. carried old photographs around that faded over time.
d. scared the other children who thought she might be a ghost.

15. "They stopped running and stood in the great jungle that covered Venus, that grew and never stopped growing, tumultuously, even as you watched it. It was a nest of octopi, clustering up great arms of fleshlike weed, wavering, flowering in this brief spring."

In these sentences, why does the author compare Venus to a jungle?

a. to describe how different it is from Earth
b. to show how Venus's plant life is affected by the brief period of sunshine
c. to show that it is like a wild and unsafe jungle for children
d. to show that there are unusual fish and other wildlife on this planet

Find Word Meanings

The five words listed below appear in "All Summer in a Day." Study the words and their definitions. Use the page numbers to check how the words are used in the story. Then complete the following sentences by using each vocabulary word only *once*.

word	meaning	page
compounded	piled up, put one on top of each other	153
slackening	letting up, getting weaker	155
surged	moved in a strong, sudden motion	156
tumultuously	in a disorganized way, randomly	157
resilient	strong, able to recover quickly	158

In "All Summer in a Day," the planet Venus is dark and rainy almost all of the time. Where I live, we get a lot of rain and snow, too. During the last strong snowstorm, the flakes fell down crazily and _____16_____. Sheets of white snow _____17_____ up against the windows because of the strong winds. Two hours later, the storm still showed no signs of _____18_____. A week after the snow stopped, it was still _____19_____, refusing to melt when the sun came out. Then another storm _____20_____ the snow on the sidewalks by dropping another six inches of snow on them. But thankfully, this kind of weather doesn't last *all* the time in my town like it does on Venus. Once the winter ends, we experience plenty of warm, sunny days!

Look at Language

Onomatopoeia

When a word *sounds* like the thing it describes, this is known as **onomatopoeia**. Some examples of onomatopoeia are *splash*, *hiss*, *crunch*, and *buzz*. Say these words softly to yourself. Notice how each *sounds* like the thing it describes. Like descriptive language, onomatopoeia helps to create a picture, or produce an effect.

Answer the following questions about onomatopoeia in "All Summer in a Day."

21. When the author writes that the children heard Margot's *muffled* cries, what sort of sound is he describing?

    a. a sound that can't be heard clearly
    b. a sound like the rain falling outside
    c. a very loud sound as Margot tries to escape
    d. a sound in the distance as the children move away

22. Which word is *not* an example of onomatopoeia?

    a. gush
    b. hiss
    c. fresh
    d. squeak

23. Which phrase from the story contains an example of onomatopoeia?

    a. "Lightning struck ten miles away . . ."
    b. "Then one of them gave a little cry."
    c. "Behind the closet door was only silence."
    d. "A boom of thunder startled them . . ."

24. Identify the phrase that contains onomatopoeia in the following sentence:

"But then they always awoke to the tatting drum, the endless shaking down of clear bead necklaces upon the roof, the walk, the gardens, the forests, and their dreams were gone."

    a. shaking down
    b. tatting drum
    c. clear bead
    d. always awoke

25. Which of the following examples of onomatopoeia BEST describes the nonstop rain on Venus?

    a. splashing
    b. whizzing
    c. jangling
    d. chattering

Review the Case

The following activities will help you review and reflect on what happened in "All Summer in a Day."

1. **Discuss.** How do you feel about what the children did to Margot? What was your reaction to what happened to her in the story?

2. **Write.** Think about something very important to you and how it makes you feel. Write a page describing your selection. Then write about how it makes you feel and about how you would feel if you couldn't have it for one or another reason.

3. Technology Application. Venus is the setting for this story. Find out more about the planet. Conduct research and then write two to three paragraphs describing what Venus is actually like. Share your information with your classmates.

"We heard you talking about your treasure."
The voice was slurred.
"We just want to see it, that's all."

The Treasure of Lemon Brown

by Walter Dean Myers

The dark sky, filled with angry, swirling clouds, reflected Greg Ridley's mood as he sat on the stoop of his building. His father's voice came to him again, first reading the letter the principal had sent to the house, then lecturing endlessly about his poor efforts in math.

"I had to leave school when I was thirteen," his father had said, "that's a year younger than you are now. If I'd had half the chances that you have, I'd . . ."

Greg had sat in the small, pale green kitchen listening, knowing the lecture would end with his father saying he couldn't play ball with the Scorpions. He had asked his father the week before, and his father had said it depended on his next report card. It wasn't often the Scorpions took on new players, especially fourteen-year-olds, and this was a chance of a lifetime for Greg. He hadn't been allowed to play high school ball, which he had really wanted to do, but playing for the Community Center team was the next best thing. Report cards were due in a week, and Greg had been hoping for the best. But the principal had ended the suspense early when she sent that letter saying Greg would probably fail math if he didn't spend more time studying.

"And you want to play basketball?" His father's brows knitted over deep brown eyes. "That must be some kind of a joke. Now you just get into your room and hit those books."

That had been two nights before. His father's words, like the distant thunder that now echoed through the streets of Harlem, still rumbled softly in his ears.

It was beginning to cool. Gusts of wind made bits of paper dance between the parked cars. There was a flash of nearby lightning, and soon large drops of rain splashed onto his jeans. He stood to go upstairs, thought of the lecture that probably awaited him if he did anything except shut himself in his room with his math book, and started walking down the street instead. Down the block there was an old tenement that had been abandoned for some months. Some of the guys had held an impromptu checker tournament there the week before, and Greg had noticed that the door, once boarded over, had been slightly ajar.

Pulling his collar up as high as he could, he checked for traffic and made a dash across the street. He reached the house just as another flash of lightning changed the night to day for an instant, then returned the graffiti-scarred building to the grim shadows. He vaulted over the outer stairs and pushed tentatively on the door. It was open, and he let himself in.

The inside of the building was dark except for the dim light that filtered through the dirty windows from the streetlamps. There was a room a few feet from the door, and from where he stood at the entrance, Greg could see a squarish patch of light on the floor. He entered the room, frowning at the musty smell. It was a large room that might have been someone's parlor at one time. Squinting, Greg could see an old table on its side against one wall, what looked like a pile of rags or a torn mattress in the corner, and a couch, with one side broken, in front of the window.

He went to the couch. The side that wasn't broken was comfortable enough, though a little creaky. From the spot he could see the blinking neon sign over the bodega on the corner. He sat awhile, watching the sign blink first green then red, allowing his mind to drift to the Scorpions, then to his father. His father had been a postal worker for all Greg's life, and was proud of it, often telling Greg how hard he had worked to pass the test. Greg had heard the story too many times to be interested now.

For a moment Greg thought he heard something that sounded

like a scraping against the wall. He listened carefully, but it was gone.

Outside the wind had picked up, sending the rain against the window with a force that shook the glass in its frame. A car passed, its tires hissing over the wet street and its red taillights glowing in the darkness.

Greg thought he heard the noise again. His stomach tightened as he held himself still and listened intently. There weren't any more scraping noises, but he was sure he had heard something in the darkness—something breathing!

He tried to figure out just where the breathing was coming from; he knew it was in the room with him. Slowly he stood, tensing. As he turned, a flash of lightning lit up the room, frightening him with its sudden brilliance. He saw nothing, just the overturned table, the pile of rags and an old newspaper on the floor. Could he have been imagining the sounds? He continued listening, but heard nothing and thought that it might have just been rats. Still, he thought, as soon as the rain let up he would leave. He went to the window and was about to look when he heard a voice behind him.

"Don't try nothin' 'cause I got a razor here sharp enough to cut a week into nine days!"

Greg, except for an involuntary tremor in his knees, stood stock still. The voice was high and brittle, like dry twigs being broken, surely not one he had ever heard before. There was a shuffling sound as the person who had been speaking moved a step closer. Greg turned, holding his breath, his eyes straining to see in the dark room.

The upper part of the figure before him was still in darkness. The lower half was in the dim rectangle of light that fell unevenly from the window. There were two feet, in cracked, dirty shoes from which rose legs that were wrapped in rags.

"Who are you?" Greg hardly recognized his own voice.

"I'm Lemon Brown," came the answer. "Who're you?"

"Greg Ridley."

"What you doing here?" The figure shuffled forward again, and Greg took a small step backward.

"It's raining," Greg said.

"I can see that," the figure said.

The person who called himself Lemon Brown peered forward, and Greg could see him clearly.

He was an old man. His black, heavily wrinkled face was surrounded by a halo of crinkly white hair and whiskers that seemed to separate his head from the layers of dirty coats piled on his smallish frame. His pants were bagged to the knee, where they were met with rags that went down to the old shoes. The rags were held on with strings, and there was a rope around his middle. Greg relaxed. He had seen the man before, picking through the trash on the corner and pulling clothes out of a Salvation Army box. There was no sign of the razor that could "cut a week into nine days."

"What are you doing here?" Greg asked.

"This is where I'm staying," Lemon Brown said. "What you here for?"

"Told you it was raining out," Greg said, leaning against the back of the couch until he felt it give slightly.

"Ain't you got no home?"

"I got a home," Greg answered.

"You ain't one of them bad boys looking for my treasure, is you?" Lemon Brown cocked his head to one side and squinted one eye. "Because I told you I got me a razor."

"I'm not looking for your treasure," Greg answered, smiling. "*If* you have one."

"What you mean, *if* I have one," Lemon Brown said. "Every man got a treasure. You don't know that, you must be a fool!"

"Sure," Greg said as he sat on the sofa and put one leg over the back. "What do you have, gold coins?"

"Don't worry none about what I got," Lemon Brown said. "You know who I am?"

"You told me your name was orange or lemon or something like that."

"Lemon Brown," the old man said, pulling back his shoulders as he did so, "they used to call me Sweet Lemon Brown."

"Sweet Lemon?" Greg asked.

"Yessir. Sweet Lemon Brown. They used to say I sung the blues so sweet that if I sang at a funeral, the dead would commence to rocking with the beat. Used to travel all over Mississippi and as far as Monroe, Louisiana, and east on over to Macon, Georgia. You mean you ain't never heard of Sweet Lemon Brown?"

"Afraid not," Greg said. "What . . . what happened to you?"

"Hard times, boy. Hard times always after a poor man. One day I got tired, sat down to rest a spell and felt a tap on my shoulder. Hard times caught up with me."

"Sorry about that."

"What you doing here? How come you didn't go on home when the rain come? Rain don't bother you young folks none."

"Just didn't." Greg looked away.

"I used to have a knotty-headed boy just like you." Lemon Brown had half walked, half shuffled back to the corner and sat down against the wall. "Had them big eyes like you got, I used to call them moon eyes. Look into them moon eyes and see anything you want."

"How come you gave up singing the blues?" Greg asked.

"Didn't give it up," Lemon Brown said. "You don't give up the blues; they give you up. After a while you do good for yourself, and it ain't nothing but foolishness singing about how hard you got it. Ain't that right?"

"I guess so."

"What's that noise?" Lemon Brown asked, suddenly sitting upright.

Greg listened, and he heard a noise outside. He looked at Lemon Brown and saw the old man pointing toward the window.

Greg went to the window and saw three men, neighborhood thugs, on the stoop. One was carrying a length of pipe. Greg looked back toward Lemon Brown, who moved quietly across the room to the window. The old man looked out, then beckoned frantically for Greg to follow him. For a moment Greg couldn't move. Then he found himself following Lemon Brown into the hallway and up darkened stairs. Greg followed as closely as he could. They reached the top of the stairs, and Greg felt Lemon Brown's hand first lying on his shoulder, then probing down his arm until he finally took Greg's hand into his own as they crouched in the darkness. "They's bad men," Lemon Brown whispered. His breath was warm against Greg's skin.

"Hey! Rag man!" A voice called. "We know you in here. What you got up under them rags? You got any money?"

Silence.

"We don't want to have to come in and hurt you, old man, but we don't mind if we have to."

Lemon Brown squeezed Greg's hand in his own hard, gnarled fist.

There was a banging downstairs and a light as the men entered. They banged around noisily, calling for the rag man.

"We heard you talking about your treasure." The voice was slurred. "We just want to see it, that's all."

"You sure he's here?" One voice seemed to come from the room with the sofa.

"Yeah, he stays here every night."

"There's another room over there; I'm going to take a look. You got that flashlight?"

"Yeah, here, take the pipe too."

Greg opened his mouth to quiet the sound of his breath as he sucked it in uneasily. A beam of light hit the wall a few feet opposite him, then went out.

"Ain't nobody in that room," a voice said. "You think he gone or something?"

"I don't know," came the answer. "All I know is that I heard him talking about some kind of treasure. You know they found that shopping bag lady with that money in her bags."

"Yeah. You think he's upstairs?"

"HEY, OLD MAN, ARE YOU UP THERE?"

Silence.

"Watch my back, I'm going up."

There was a footstep on the stairs, and the beam from the flashlight danced crazily along the peeling wallpaper. Greg held his breath. There was another step and a loud crashing noise as the man banged the pipe against the wooden banister. Greg could feel his temples throb as the man slowly neared them. Greg thought about the pipe, wondering what he would do when the man reached them—what he *could* do.

Then Lemon Brown released his hand and moved toward the top of the stairs. Greg looked around and saw stairs going up to the next floor. He tried waving to Lemon Brown, hoping the old man would see him in the dim light and follow him to the next floor.

Maybe, Greg thought, the man wouldn't follow them up there. Suddenly, though, Lemon Brown stood at the top of the stairs, both arms raised high above his head.

"There he is!" A voice cried from below.

"Throw down your money, old man, so I won't have to bash your head in!"

Now it's time for YOU to be the Reader as Detective.

Lemon Brown and Greg seem to be in a very dangerous situation. How do you think they will get themselves out of it, if at all?

Read the rest of the story to see what happens to Lemon Brown and Greg next.

Lemon Brown didn't move. Greg felt himself near panic. The steps came closer, and still Lemon Brown didn't move. He was an eerie sight, a bundle of rags standing at the top of the stairs, his shadow on the wall looming over him. Maybe, the thought came to Greg, the scene could be even eerier.

Greg wet his lips, put his hands to his mouth and tried to make a sound. Nothing came out. He swallowed hard, wet his lips once more and howled as evenly as he could.

"What's that?"

As Greg howled, the light moved away from Lemon Brown, but not before Greg saw him hurl his body down the stairs at the men who had come to take his treasure. There was a crashing noise, and then footsteps. A rush of warm air came in as the downstairs door opened, then there was only an ominous silence.

Greg stood on the landing. He listened, and after a while there was another sound on the staircase.

"Mr. Brown?" he called.

"Yeah, it's me," came the answer. "I got their flashlight."

Greg exhaled in relief as Lemon Brown made his way slowly back up the stairs.

"You OK?"

"Few bumps and bruises," Lemon Brown said.

"I think I'd better be going," Greg said, his breath returning to normal. "You'd better leave, too, before they come back."

"They may hang around outside for a while," Lemon Brown said, "but they ain't getting their nerve up to come in here again. Not with crazy old rag men and howling spooks. Best you stay a while till the coast is clear. I'm heading out west tomorrow, out to east St. Louis."

"They were talking about treasures," Greg said. "You really have a treasure?"

"What I tell you? Didn't I tell you every man got a treasure?" Lemon Brown said. "You want to see mine?"

"If you want to show it to me," Greg shrugged.

"Let's look out the window first, see what them scoundrels be doing," Lemon Brown said.

They followed the oval beam of the flashlight into one of the rooms and looked out the window. They saw the men who had tried to take the treasure sitting on the curb near the corner. One of them had his pants leg up, looking at his knee.

"You sure you're not hurt?" Greg asked Lemon Brown.

"Nothing that ain't been hurt before," Lemon Brown said. "When you get as old as me all you say when something hurts is, 'Howdy, Mr. Pain, sees you back again.' Then when Mr. Pain see he can't worry you none, he go on mess with somebody else."

Greg smiled.

"Here, you hold this." Lemon Brown gave Greg the flashlight.

He sat on the floor near Greg and carefully untied the strings that held the rags on his right leg. When he took the rags away, Greg saw a piece of plastic. The old man carefully took off the plastic and unfolded it. He revealed some yellowed newspaper clippings and a battered harmonica.

"There it be," he said, nodding his head. "There it be."

Greg looked at the old man, saw the distant look in his eye, then turned to the clippings. They told of Sweet Lemon Brown, a blues singer and harmonica player who was appearing at different theaters in the South. One of the clippings said he had been the hit of the show, although not the headliner. All of the clippings were reviews of shows Lemon Brown had been in more than 50 years ago. Greg looked at the harmonica. It was dented badly on one side, with the reed holes on one end nearly closed.

"I used to travel around and make money to feed my wife and Jesse— that's my boy's name. Used to feed them good, too. Then his mama died, and he stayed with his mama's sister. He growed up

to be a man, and when the war come he saw fit to go off and fight in it. I didn't have nothing to give him except these things that told him who I was, and what he come from. If you know your pappy did something, you know you can do something too.

"Anyway, he went off to war, and I went off still playing and singing. 'Course by then I wasn't as much as I used to be, not without somebody to make it worth the while. You know what I mean?"

"Yeah," Greg nodded, not quite really knowing.

"I traveled around, and one time I come home, and there was this letter saying Jesse got killed in the war. Broke my heart, it truly did.

"They sent back what he had with him over there, and what it was is this old mouth fiddle and these clippings. Him carrying it around with him like that told me it meant something to him. That was my treasure, and when I give it to him he treated it just like that, a treasure. Ain't that something?"

"Yeah, I guess so," Greg said.

"You *guess* so?" Lemon Brown's voice rose an octave as he started to put his treasure back into the plastic. "Well, you got to guess 'cause you sure don't know nothing. Don't know enough to get home when it's raining."

"I guess . . . I mean, you're right."

"You OK for a youngster," the old man said as he tied the strings around his leg, "better than those scalawags what come here looking for my treasure. That's for sure."

"You really think that treasure of yours was worth fighting for?" Greg asked. "Against a pipe?"

"What else a man got 'cepting what he can pass on to his son, or his daughter, if she be his oldest?" Lemon Brown said. "For a big-headed boy you sure do ask the foolishest questions."

Lemon Brown got up after patting his rags in place and looked out the window again.

"Looks like they're gone. You get on out of here and get yourself home. I'll be watching from the window so you'll be all right."

Lemon Brown went down the stairs behind Greg. When they reached the front door the old man looked out first, saw the street was clear and told Greg to scoot on home.

"You sure you'll be OK?" Greg asked.

"Now didn't I tell you I was going to east St. Louis in the morning?" Lemon Brown asked. "Don't that sound OK to you?"

"Sure it does," Greg said. "Sure it does. And you take care of that treasure of yours."

"That I'll do," Lemon said, the wrinkles about his eyes suggesting a smile. "That I'll do."

The night had warmed and the rain had stopped, leaving puddles at the curbs. Greg didn't even want to think how late it was. He thought ahead of what his father would say and wondered if he should tell him about Lemon Brown. He thought about it until he reached his stoop, and decided against it. Lemon Brown would be OK, Greg thought, with his memories and his treasure.

Greg pushed the button over the bell marked Ridley, thought of the lecture he knew his father would give him, and smiled.

Be a Reading Detective

Read each of the following questions. Then write the letter of the correct answer to each question. Remember, the symbol next to each question identifies the *kind* of reading skill that particular question helps you to develop.

1. This story is mainly about

    a. finding shelter in a rainstorm.

    b. the value of a person's life.

    c. learning to survive on the streets.

    d. spending time with friends and family.

2. What happened right before Greg left home?

   a. Greg got into a huge fight with his dad.

   b. Greg was remembering an argument with his dad.

   c. Greg found out he failed a math test.

   d. Greg was removed from the high school team.

3. Why did Greg come out of his hiding place and start howling?

   a. He was too scared to keep quiet any longer.

   b. He wanted the group of men to think he was a ghost.

   c. He thought the men were going to come up the stairs.

   d. He was trying to get Lemon Brown's attention.

4. "Slowly he stood, tensing. As he turned, a flash of lightning lit up the room, frightening him with its sudden brilliance." In this context, *brilliance* means

   a. intelligence.

   b. brightness.

   c. loudness.

   d. danger.

5. Which line from the story is an opinion?

   a. "You told me your name was orange or lemon or something like that."

   b. "We heard you talking about your treasure."

   c. "Hard times always after a poor man."

   d. "They sent back what he had with him over there . . ."

6. What is Lemon Brown's treasure?

   a. newspaper clippings and a harmonica

   b. a collection of gold coins

   c. a medal his son won

   d. a photograph of his wife

7. From page 170 of the story, we can probably infer that Lemon Brown is

a. homeless.
b. crazy.
c. depressed.
d. angry.

8. What are Lemon Brown's plans?

a. to keep coming back to the house
b. to sell his treasure
c. to go to St. Louis the next day
d. to teach the neighborhood thugs a lesson

9. What will most likely happen once Greg gets home?

a. He will tell his dad about Lemon Brown.
b. He will start keeping a treasure of his own.
c. He will listen to some music like Lemon Brown used to play.
d. He will get a lecture from his dad.

10. Which statement about the characters is a fact?

a. Lemon Brown's treasure is not worth much money.
b. Greg should have more respect for his father's values.
c. The men who come into the house are probably unhappy.
d. Lemon Brown's son should not have joined the army.

Follow the Trail

Mood

Mood in a story refers to the feeling the story creates in the reader. Authors use descriptive language, often when they are describing the setting of a story, to create a specific mood.

The following questions will give you practice identifying mood in "The Treasure of Lemon Brown."

11. When Greg and Lemon Brown first meet (top of page 170), the feeling or mood between them is
  a. friendly.
  b. tense.
  c. furious.
  d. neutral.

12. How does the rain in the story contribute to the overall mood?
  a. It sounds like the rhythms of Lemon Brown's music.
  b. It shows that neither of the characters is happy.
  c. It helps make the house dark and scary.
  d. It is the reason the two main characters are in the house.

13. "Greg listened, and he heard a noise outside. He looked at Lemon Brown and saw the old man pointing toward the window." This paragraph is intended to make the reader feel
  a. excited.
  b. curious.
  c. angry.
  d. surprised.

14. Which phrase from page 169 best shows the creepy mood the author creates?
  a. "might have just been rats"
  b. "something breathing"
  c. "wrapped in rags"
  d. "eyes straining to see"

15. How does the mood change in the second-to-last paragraph of the story?
  a. It becomes less scary and more hopeful.
  b. It becomes creepier as Greg heads home.
  c. It becomes tense because Greg has to face his father.
  d. It becomes more thoughtful because the story is about to end.

Find Word Meanings

The five words listed below appear in "The Treasure of Lemon Brown." Study the words and their definitions. Use the page numbers to check how the words are used in the story. Then complete the following sentences by using each vocabulary word only *once*.

word	meaning	page
commence	begin; start	171
beckoned	motioned or gestured to come nearer	171
probing	searching; exploring	171
gnarled	curled up unnaturally; bent; twisted	172
ominous	scary; giving a feeling that something is happening or is about to happen	173

It was a rainy day, and the dark clouds were _____16_____, indicating that something bad might _____17_____ .

Greg left home and walked down the street. He was _____18_____ around inside an abandoned building when he heard someone breathing. A man appeared and introduced himself as Lemon Brown. Greg and Lemon Brown began talking, but they were soon interrupted by the sound of intruders. Greg was afraid, but Lemon Brown protected him. Lemon Brown _____19_____ for Greg to come with him, and he took Greg's young hand in his own _____20_____ fist. The intruders left. Greg and Lemon Brown had a little more time to talk and learn from one another before going their separate ways.

Look at Language

Descriptive Language

Remember that writers use vivid, **descriptive language** to bring a story alive for readers.

Answer the following questions about descriptive language in "The Treasure of Lemon Brown."

21. Read these sentences from the story:

"'Sure,' Greg said as he sat on the sofa and put one leg over the back. 'What do you have, gold coins?'"

The description of Greg sitting on the couch reveals that he is

a. feeling nervous and on edge around Lemon Brown.
b. trying to take Lemon Brown's belongings.
c. planning to spend the night so he doesn't have to go home.
d. growing comfortable and confident around Lemon Brown.

22. Read this sentence from the story:

"'Lemon Brown,' the old man said, pulling back his shoulders as he did so, 'they used to call me Sweet Lemon Brown.'"

What does Lemon Brown's stance (the way he holds his shoulders) say about him?

a. He is proud to tell Greg that he was known as Sweet Lemon Brown.
b. He is guarded and shy around Greg.
c. He is annoyed that Greg is asking so many questions.
d. He is growing weak in his old age.

23. "'Hard times always after a poor man. One day I got tired, sat down to rest a spell and felt a tap on my shoulder. Hard times caught up with me.'"

In these descriptive sentences, what is Lemon Brown saying about life?

a. A poor man is always going to be hit with difficult times in life.

b. Your own choices affect whether you have a tough or easy life.

c. It's tough to sleep at night without someone tapping and waking you.

d. A poor man can avoid hardships if he tries hard enough.

24. "'When you get as old as me all you can say when something hurts is, "Howdy, Mr. Pain, sees you back again." Then when Mr. Pain see he can't worry you none, he go on mess with somebody else.'"

In these descriptive sentences, what is Lemon Brown saying about getting older?

a. Pain and suffering are unavoidable.

b. It is frustrating that you get injured more often.

c. Pain doesn't bother you if you don't let it.

d. Your body doesn't hurt as much as when you're young.

25. "Greg looked at the old man, saw the distant look in his eye, then turned to the clippings."

Why does the author write that the old man has a distant look in his eye when he takes out the newspaper clippings?

a. Lemon Brown is lost in thoughts about his past.

b. Lemon Brown is growing bored with of his conversation with Greg.

c. Lemon Brown is thinking about other places he'd rather be.

d. Lemon Brown is getting upset that Greg is so nosey.

Review the Case

The following activities will help you review and reflect on what happened in "The Treasure of Lemon Brown."

1. Discuss. Music that is classified as the blues usually expresses feelings about hardships, such as loneliness or bad luck. Why might it be appropriate for Lemon Brown to be singing the blues?

2. **Write.** Lemon Brown is most likely homeless in the story. There are various reasons a person could become homeless, some that you might not expect. Do some research and try to find some of the most common causes for homelessness. Prepare a bullet-point list of at least three causes. Explain each point.

3. **Technology Application.** Get a sense of what kind of music Lemon Brown used to sing. Find audio (sound) or video sources of blues music and listen to a few songs. How does the music make you feel? Can you imagine Lemon Brown singing it with a band? Discuss your answers with your classmates.

**"Oh," Arnie stuttered. "Actually, my cousin
José really does the work and I kind of,
you know, supervise."**

Born Worker

PART I

by Gary Soto

They said that José was born with a ring of dirt around his
neck, with grime under his fingernails, and skin calloused from the
grainy twist of a shovel. They said his palms were already rough by
the time he was three, and soon after he learned his primary colors, his squint was the squint of an aged laborer. They said he was
a born worker. By seven he was drinking coffee slowly, his mouth
pursed the way his mother sipped. He wore jeans, a shirt with
sleeves rolled to his elbows. His eye could measure a length of
board, and his knees genuflected over flower beds and leafy gutters.

They said lots of things about José, but almost nothing of his
parents. His mother stitched at a machine all day, and his father,
with a steady job at the telephone company, climbed splintered,
sun-sucked poles, fixed wires and looked around the city at tree
level.

"What do you see up there?" José once asked his father.

"Work," he answered. "I see years of work, *mi'jo*."

José took this as a truth, and though he did well in school, he
felt destined to labor. His arms would pump, his legs would bend,
his arms would carry a world of earth. He believed in hard work,
believed that his strength was as ancient as a rock's.

"Life is hard," his father repeated from the time José could first make out the meaning of words until he was stroking his fingers against the grain of his sandpaper beard.

His mother was an example to José. She would raise her hands, showing her fingers pierced from the sewing machines. She bled on her machine, bled because there was money to make, a child to raise, and a roof to stay under.

One day when José returned home from junior high, his cousin Arnie was sitting on the lawn sucking on a stalk of grass. José knew that grass didn't come from his lawn. His was cut and pampered, clean.

"José!" Arnie shouted as he took off the earphones of his CD Walkman.

"Hi, Arnie," José said without much enthusiasm.

He didn't like his cousin. He thought he was lazy and, worse, spoiled by the trappings of being middle class. His parents had good jobs in offices and showered him with clothes, shoes, CDs, vacations, almost anything he wanted. Arnie's family had never climbed a telephone pole to size up the future.

Arnie rose to his feet, and José saw that his cousin was wearing a new pair of high-tops. He didn't say anything.

"Got an idea," Arnie said cheerfully. "Something that'll make us money."

José looked at his cousin, not a muscle of curiosity twitching in his face.

Still, Arnie explained that since he himself was so clever with words, and his best cousin in the whole world was good at working with his hands, that maybe they might start a company.

"What would you do?" José asked.

"Me?" he said brightly. "Shoot, I'll round up all kinds of jobs for you. You won't have to do anything." He stopped, then started again. "Except—you know—do the work." .

"Get out of here," José said.

"Don't be that way," Arnie begged. "Let me tell you how it works."

The boys went inside the house, and while José stripped off his school clothes and put on his jeans and a T-shirt, Arnie told him that they could be rich.

"You ever hear of this guy named Bechtel? Arnie asked.

José shook his head.

"Man, he started just like us," Arnie said. "He started digging ditches and stuff, and the next thing you knew, he was sitting by his own swimming pool. You want to sit by your own pool, don't you?" Arnie smiled, waiting for José to speak up.

"Never heard of this guy Bechtel," José said after he rolled on two huge socks, worn at the heels. He opened up his chest of drawers and brought out a packet of Kleenex.

Arnie looked at the Kleenex.

"How come you don't use your sleeve?" Arnie joked.

José thought a moment and said, "I'm not like you." He smiled at his retort.

"Listen, I'll find the work, and then we can split it fifty-fifty."

José knew fifty-fifty was a bad deal.

"How about sixty-forty?" Arnie suggested when he could see that José wasn't going for it. "I know a lot of people from my dad's job. They're waiting for us."

José sat on the edge of his bed and started to lace up his boots. He knew that there were agencies that would find you work, agencies

 that took a portion of your pay. They're cheats, he thought, people who sit in air-conditioned offices while others work.

"You really know a lot of people?" José asked.

"Boatloads," Arnie said, "My dad works with this millionaire—honest—who cooks a steak for his dog every day."

He's a liar, José thought. No matter how he tried he couldn't picture a dog grubbing on steak. The world was too poor for that kind of silliness.

"Listen, I'll go eighty-twenty," José said.

"Aw, man," Arnie whined. "That ain't fair."

José laughed.

"I mean, half the work is finding the jobs," Arnie explained, his palms up as he begged José to be reasonable.

José knew this was true. He had had to go door-to-door, and he disliked asking for work. He assumed that it should automatically be his since he was a good worker, honest, and always on time.

"Where did you get this idea, anyhow?" José asked.

"I got a business mind," Arnie said proudly.

"Just like that Bechtel guy," José retorted.

"That's right."

José agreed to a seventy-thirty split, with the condition that Arnie had to help out. Arnie hollered, arguing that some people were meant to work and others to come up with brilliant ideas. He was one of the latter. Still, he agreed after José said it was that or nothing.

In the next two weeks, Arnie found an array of jobs. José peeled off shingles from a rickety garage roof, carried rocks down a path to where a pond would go, and spray-painted lawn furniture. And while Arnie accompanied him, most of the time he did nothing. He did help occasionally. He did shake the cans of spray paint and kick aside debris so that José didn't trip while going down the path carrying the rocks. He did stack the piles of shingles, but almost cried when a nail bit his thumb. But mostly he told José what he had missed or where the work could be improved. José was bothered because he and his work had never been criticized before.

But soon José learned to ignore his cousin, ignore his comments about his spray painting, or about the way he lugged rocks, two in each arm. He didn't say anything, either, when they got paid and Arnie rubbed his hands like a fly, muttering, "It's payday."

Then Arnie found a job scrubbing a drained swimming pool. The two boys met early at José's house. Arnie brought his bike. José's own bike had a flat and grinned like a clown's face.

"I'll pedal," José suggested when Arnie said that he didn't have much leg strength.

With Arnie on the handlebars, José tore off, his pedaling so strong that tears of fear formed in Arnie's eyes.

"Slow down!" Arnie cried.

José ignored him and within minutes they were riding the bike up a gravel driveway. Arnie hopped off at first chance.

"You're scary," Arnie said, picking a gnat from his eye.

José chuckled.

When Arnie knocked on the door, an old man still in pajamas appeared in the window. He motioned for the boys to come around to the back.

"Let me do the talking," Arnie suggested to his cousin. "He knows my dad real good. They're like this." He pressed two fingers together.

José didn't bother to say OK. He walked the bike into the back-yard, which was lush with plants—roses in their last bloom, gerani-ums, hydrangeas, pansies with their skirts of bright colors. José could make out the splash of a fountain. Then he heard the hysterical yapping of a poodle. From all his noise, a person might have thought the dog was on fire.

"Hi, Mr. Clemens," Arnie said, extending his hand. "I'm Arnie Sanchez. It's nice to see you again."

José had never seen a kid actually greet someone like this. Mr. Clemens said, hiking up his pajama bottoms, "I only wanted one kid to work."

"Oh," Arnie stuttered. "Actually, my cousin José really does the work and I kind of, you know, supervise."

Mr. Clemens pinched up his wrinkled face. He seemed not to understand. He took out a pea-sized hearing aid, fiddled with its tiny dial, and fit it into his ear, which was surrounded with wiry gray hair.

"I'm only paying for one boy," Mr. Clemens shouted. His poodle click-clicked and stood behind his legs. The dog bared its small crooked teeth.

"That's right," Arnie said, smiling a strained smile. "We know that you're going to compensate only one of us."

Mr. Clemens muttered under his breath. He combed his hair with his fingers. He showed José the pool, which was shaped as round as an elephant. It was filthy with grime. Near the bottom some grayish water shimmered and leaves floated as limp as cornflakes.

"It's got to be real clean," Mr. Clemens said, "or it's not worth it."

"Oh, José's a great worker," Arnie said. He patted his cousin's shoulders and said that he could lift a mule.

Mr. Clemens sized up José and squeezed his shoulders, too.

"How do I know you, anyhow?" Mr. Clemens asked Arnie, who was aiming a smile at the poodle.

"You know my dad," Arnie answered, raising his smile to the old man. "He works at Interstate Insurance. You and he had some business deals."

Mr. Clemens thought for a moment, a hand on his mouth, head shaking. He could have been thinking about the meaning of life, his face was so dark.

"Mexican fella?" he inquired.

"That's him," Arnie said happily.

José felt like hitting his cousin for his cheerful attitude. Instead, he walked over and picked up the white plastic bottle of bleach. Next to it were a wire brush, a pumice stone, and some rags. He set down the bottle and, like a surgeon, put on a pair of rubber gloves.

"You know what you're doing, boy?" Mr. Clemens asked.

José nodded as he walked into the pool. If it had been filled with water, his chest would have been wet. The new hair on his chest would have been floating like the legs of a jelly-fish.

"Oh yeah," Arnie chimed, speaking for his cousin. "José was born to work."

José would have drowned his cousin if there had been more water. Instead, he poured a bleach solution into a rag and swirled it over an area. He took the wire brush and scrubbed. The black algae came up like a foamy monster.

"We're a team," Arnie said to Mr. Clemens.

Arnie descended into the pool and took the bleach bottle from José. He held it for José and smiled up at Mr. Clemens, who, hands on hips, watched for a while, the poodle at his side. He cupped his ear, as if to pick up the sound of José's scrubbing.

"Nice day, huh?" Arnie sang.

"What?" Mr. Clemens said.

"Nice day," Arnie repeated, this time louder. "So which ear can't you hear in?" Grinning, Arnie wiggled his ear to make sure that Mr. Clemens knew what he was asking.

Mr. Clemens ignored Arnie. He watched José, whose arms worked back and forth like he was sawing logs.

"We're not only a team," Arnie shouted, "but we're also cousins."

Mr. Clemens shook his head at Arnie. When he left, the poo-dle leading the way, Arnie immediately climbed out of the pool and sat on the edge, legs dangling.

Now it's time for YOU to be the Reader as Detective.

You've met the three main characters in the story—José, Arnie, and Mr. Clemens. You also know where the story takes place. Can you predict what might happen in Part 2?

Be a Reading Detective

Read each of the following questions. Then write the letter of the correct answer to each question. Remember, the symbol next to each question identifies the *kind* of reading skill that particular question helps you to develop.

1. This first part of the story is mainly about

   a. Arnie and José teaming up to get jobs.

   b. Arnie acting superior to José.

   c. José working hard to get ahead.

   d. the values José's parents have taught him.

2. When Arnie tells José he wants to start a company, José asks "What would you do?" Why might this be José's first question?

   a. He suspects that Arnie is going to give himself an easier role.

   b. He thinks it sounds like a great idea.

   c. He wonders what steps Arnie will take to make it happen.

   d. He is concerned that Arnie is trying to take on too much at once.

3. Why will José not agree to a fifty-fifty deal? Why does he think it's not fair?

   a. He doesn't like his cousin very much.

   b. He doesn't think Arnie will find them any work.

    c. He knows he will do much more than half the work.

    d. José wants to show Arnie just how spoiled he is.

4. According to Arnie, who is Bechtel?

    a. somebody who worked hard and became rich

    b. a man who sells insurance with his father

    c. the head of an agency who finds work for people

    d. a neighbor who has hired the boys to do a job

5. "José thought a moment and said, "'I'm not like you.' He smiled at his retort."

    What is another way to say *retort*?

    a. funny remark

    b. sharp response

    c. friendly greeting

    d. curious question

6. Which is one of the ways Arnie tries to convince his cousin to work with him?

    a. He tells José he can get new high-tops with the money he makes.

    b. He promises that he will do all the hard work.

    c. He tells José he already has some jobs scheduled.

    d. He says José is his best cousin in the whole world.

7. What is the main idea the author is trying to convey on page 187?

    a. José is doing the heavy work while Arnie watches.

    b. Arnie is making sure that José always does a good job.

    c. The boys are working together on a lot of different jobs.

    d. José cares more than Arnie does about getting the job done.

8. "'That's right,' Arnie said, smiling a strained smile. 'We know that you're going to compensate only one of us.'" What does *compensate* mean here?

   a. pay
   b. watch
   c. use
   d. know

9. Which happens second?

   a. Arnie suggests that he and José work together.
   b. Arnie and José meet Mr. Clemens.
   c. José wishes he could drown Arnie in the pool.
   d. Arnie rides on the handlebars of his bike while José pedals.

10. Which sentence from the story is *not* a fact?

   a. "She would raise her hands, showing fingers pierced from the sewing machines."
   b. "They're cheats, he thought, people who sit in air-conditioned offices while others work."
   c. "José knew that grass didn't come from his lawn."
   d. "José had never seen a kid actually greet someone like this."

Follow the Trail

Characters

As you've learned, it is important to recognize and understand the different characters in a story. The following questions will help you practice this skill.

11. What is the author most likely trying to say about José in the first part of the story?

    a. José enjoys working hard and wants to keep doing it until he's old.

    b. José looks and acts like he's an adult, like he's been working for many years.

    c. When José is busy working, he looks exactly like his mom and dad.

    d. José looks like a hard worker so people treat him like one.

12. Why does the author include details about the hard work José's parents do?

    a. to show that José someday wants to climb telephone poles

    b. to show that everyone in José's family likes to work

    c. to show that José's parents aren't like Arnie's parents

    d. to show what kind of future José expects to have

13. Why does José dislike going door-to-door to ask for work?

    a. He feels he deserves the work and shouldn't have to ask for it.

    b. He's too shy to approach people.

    c. He doesn't know if he would do a good enough job.

    d. He's afraid to bother people in their homes.

14. "He set down the bottle and, like a surgeon, put on a pair of rubber gloves." This tells you that José is

    a. experienced in hospital work.

    b. afraid to get dirty.

    c. very precise and careful.

    d. scared of getting sick.

15. Why does José believe that his "strength is as ancient as a rock"?

    a. His body feels old from all of the physical labor he's done.

    b. His work ethic has run in his family for years.

    c. He is strong enough to move the oldest, heaviest objects.

    d. He is in junior high and is starting to feel old.

Find Word Meanings

The five words listed below appear in "Born Worker," Part 1. Study the words and their definitions. Use the page numbers to check how the words are used in the story. Then complete the following sentences by using each vocabulary word only *once*.

word	meaning	page
genuflected	bent knees or bowed down on one knee	184
array	collection, assortment	187
debris	broken pieces, leftover bits of unwanted substances	187
supervise	watch over, be in charge of	188
descended	moved down from a higher position	189

Have you ever worked on a project with someone who made you do all of the work? I once held a bake sale with my classmate Jessica. We were trying to raise money for new soccer uniforms. Jessica, like Arnie in "Born Worker," preferred to give orders and _____16_____ rather than do any of the work herself. I did everything—I made the fliers, hung them around the school, and baked a nice _____17_____ of desserts, including brownies, cookies, and cupcakes. She just watched and made comments. The worst was when my four-year-old brother accidentally knocked over a tray of fudge brownies. Jessica started yelling about how we wouldn't have enough food to sell. I calmly _____18_____ to pick up the brownies and clean the mess. We had to throw them out because they got dirty from all the dirt and _____19_____ on the floor. But luckily, I remembered that my mom had an extra box of brownie mix in our basement. I _____20_____ into the basement storage room, found the box, and made a new batch. Problem solved. We ended up with plenty of desserts to sell, and we made a good amount of money. But next time, I'm not working with Jessica!

Look at Language

Synonyms

As you know, **synonyms** are words that share the same meaning, such as *happy* and *joyous*. Use your knowledge of synonyms to answer the following questions.

21. "José took this as a truth, and though he did well in school, he felt destined to labor." A synonym for *destined* is
   a. hopeful.
   b. determined.
   c. fated.
   d. forced.

22. "But soon José learned to ignore his cousin, ignore his comments about his spray painting, or about the way he lugged rocks, two in each arm." A synonym for *lugged* is
   a. pushed.
   b. carried.
   c. dropped.
   d. dumped.

23. "'Mexican fella?' he inquired." A synonym for *inquired* is
   a. thought.
   b. questioned.
   c. denied.
   d. demanded.

24. "Near the bottom some grayish water shimmered and leaves floated as limp as cornflakes." What is a synonym for *limp* in this sentence?
   a. droopy
   b. firm
   c. colorful
   d. tempting

25. Which is a synonym for *hiking* on page 188?
   a. walking
   b. climbing
   c. pulling
   d. tying

Review the Case

The following activities will help you review and reflect on what happened in "Born Worker," Part 1.

1. Discuss. When Arnie tries to strike a deal with José, the boys go back and forth about how much money each of them should get for the work they do. Based on what you read in the story, and on your own experience, how much value is there to the work Arnie would do to find the jobs? How important is that step in the process? What share should he fairly be getting? Explain your reasoning.

2. Write. Pretend you're Arnie. You want to convince your cousin to start a business with you, and you think it would be more professional to propose your plan in writing. Write a letter to José explaining your idea for the business, how the two of you would work together, and how much each of you would get paid.

3. Technology Application. Young adults, like Arnie and José, can go into business for themselves instead of getting jobs like waiting tables or working in retail stores. Go online to a Web site like Teen Business Link (www.sba.gov/teens) and research how to start a business. Write a brief description of a business that you would be able to create and that you would enjoy. Describe what kind of time and resources would be involved.

Born Worker

PART 2

"It's going to be blazing," Arnie complained. He shaded his eyes with his hand and looked east, where the sun was rising over a sycamore, its leaves hanging like bats.

José scrubbed. He worked the wire brush over the black and green stains, the grime dripping like tears. He finished a large area. He hopped out of the pool and returned hauling a garden hose with an attached nozzle. He gave the cleaned area a blast. When the spray got too close, his cousin screamed, got up, and, searching for something to do, picked a loquat from a tree.

"What's your favorite fruit?" Arnie asked.

José ignored him.

Arnie stuffed a bunch of loquats into his mouth, then cursed himself for splattering juice on his new high-tops. He returned to the pool, his cheeks fat with the seeds, and once again sat at the edge. He started to tell José how he had first learned to swim. "We were on vacation in Mazatlán. You been there, ain't you?"

José shook his head. He dabbed the bleach solution onto the sides of the pool with a rag and scrubbed a new area.

"Anyhow, my dad was on the beach and saw this drowned dead guy," Arnie continued. "And right there, my dad got scared and realized I couldn't swim."

Arnie rattled on about how his father had taught him in the hotel pool and later showed him where the drowned man's body had been.

"Be quiet," José said.

"What?"

"I can't concentrate," José said, stepping back to look at the cleaned area.

Arnie shut his mouth but opened it to lick loquat juice from his fingers. He kicked his legs against the swimming pool, bored. He looked around the backyard and spotted a lounge chair. He got up, dusting off the back of his pants, and threw himself into the cushions. He raised and lowered the back of the lounge. Sighing, he snuggled in. He stayed quiet for three minutes, during which time José scrubbed. His arms hurt but he kept working with long strokes. José knew that in an hour the sun would drench the pool with light. He hurried to get the job done.

Arnie then asked, "You ever peel before?"

José looked at his cousin. His nose burned from the bleach. He scrunched up his face.

"You know, like when you get sunburned."

"I'm too dark to peel," José said, his words echoing because he had advanced to the deep end. "Why don't you be quiet and let me work?"

Arnie babbled on that he had peeled when on vacation in Hawaii. He explained that he was really more French than Mexican, and that's why his skin was sensitive. He said that when he lived in France, people thought that he could be Portuguese or maybe Armenian, never Mexican.

José felt like soaking his rag with bleach and pressing it over Arnie's mouth to make him be quiet.

Then Mr. Clemens appeared. He was dressed in white pants and a flowery shirt. His thin hair was combed so that his scalp, as pink as a crab, showed.

"I'm just taking a little rest," Arnie said.

Arnie leaped back into the pool. He took the bleach bottle and held it. He smiled at Mr. Clemens, who came to inspect their progress.

"José's doing a good job," Arnie said, then whistled a song.

Mr. Clemens peered into the pool, hands on knees, admiring the progress.

"Pretty good, huh?" Arnie asked.

Mr. Clemens nodded. Then his hearing aid fell out, and José turned in time to see it roll like a bottle cap toward the bottom of the pool. It leaped into the stagnant water with a plop. A single bubble went up, and it was gone.

"Dang," Mr. Clemens swore. He took shuffling steps toward the deep end. He steadied his gaze on where the hearing aid had sunk. He leaned over and suddenly, arms waving, one leg kicking out, he tumbled into the pool. He landed standing up, then his legs buckled, and he crumbled, his head striking against the bottom. He rolled once, and half of his body settled in the water.

"Did you see that!" Arnie shouted, big-eyed.

Now it's time for YOU to be the Reader as Detective.

How do you think José will react to what happened to Mr. Clemens? How do you think Arnie will react?

Read the rest of the story to find out.

José had already dropped his brushes on the side of the pool and hurried to the old man, who moaned, eyes closed, his false teeth jutting from his mouth. A ribbon of blood immediately began to flow from his scalp.

"We better get out of here!" Arnie suggested. "They're going to blame us!"

José knelt on both knees at the old man's side. He took the man's teeth from his mouth and placed them in his shirt pocket. The old man groaned and opened his eyes, which were shiny wet. He appeared startled, like a newborn.

"Sir, you'll be all right," José cooed, then snapped at his cousin. "Arnie, get over here and help me!"

"I'm going home," Arnie whined.

"You punk!" José yelled. "Go inside and call 911."

Arnie said that they should leave him there.

"Why should we get involved?" he cried as he started for his bike. "It's his own fault."

José laid the man's head down and with giant steps leaped out of the pool, shoving his cousin as he passed. He went into the kitchen and punched in 911 on a telephone. He explained to the operator what had happened. When asked the address, José dropped the phone and went onto the front porch to look for it.

"It's 940 East Brown," José breathed. He hung up and looked wildly about the kitchen. He opened up the refrigerator and brought out a plastic tray of ice, which he twisted so that a few of the cubes popped out and slid across the floor. He wrapped some cubes in a dish towel. When he raced outside, Arnie was gone, the yapping poodle was doing laps around the edge of the pool, and Mr. Clemens was trying to stand up.

"No, sir," José said as he jumped into the pool, his own knees almost buckling. "Please, sit down."

Mr. Clemens staggered and collapsed. José caught him before he hit his head again. The towel of ice cubes dropped from his hands. With his legs spread to absorb the weight, José raised the man up in his arms, this fragile man. He picked him up and carefully stepped toward the shallow end, one slow elephant step at a time.

"You'll be all right," José said, more to himself than to Mr. Clemens, who moaned and struggled to be let free.

The sirens wailed in the distance. The poodle yapped, which started a dog barking in the neighbor's yard.

"You'll be OK," José repeated, and in the shallow end of the pool, he edged up the steps. He lay the old man in the lounge chair and raced back inside for more ice and another towel. He returned outside and placed the bundle of cubes on the man's head, where the blood flowed. Mr. Clemens was awake, looking about. When the old man felt his mouth, José reached into his shirt pocket and pulled out his false teeth. He fit the teeth into Mr. Clemens's mouth and a smile appeared, something bright at a difficult time.

"I hit my head," Mr. Clemens said after smacking his teeth so that the fit was right.

José looked up and his gaze floated to a telephone pole, one his father might have climbed. If he had been there, his father would have seen that José was more than just a good worker. He would have seen a good man. He held the towel to the old man's head. The poodle, now quiet, joined them on the lounge chair.

A fire truck pulled into the driveway and soon they were surrounded by firemen, one of whom brought out a first-aid kit. A fireman led José away and asked what had happened. He was starting to explain when his cousin reappeared, yapping like a poodle.

"I was scrubbing the pool," Arnie shouted, "and I said, 'Mr. Clemens, you shouldn't stand so close to the edge.' But did he listen? No, he leaned over and . . . Well, you can just imagine my horror."

José walked away from Arnie's jabbering. He walked away, and realized that there were people like his cousin, the liar, and people like himself, someone he was getting to know. He walked and in the midmorning heat boosted himself up a telephone pole. He climbed up and saw for himself what his father saw—miles and miles of trees and houses, and a future lost in the layers of yellowish haze.

Be a Reading Detective

Read each of the following questions. Then write the letter of the correct answer to each question. Remember, the symbol next to each question identifies the *kind* of reading skill that particular question helps you to develop.

1. The second part of this story is mainly about
   a. Mr. Clemens falling in the pool and José getting help.
   b. José resenting Arnie for his irresponsible behavior.
   c. José doing a great job of cleaning the pool.
   d. The boys trying to cover up the way Mr. Clemens hurt himself.

2. Based on the information in the story, a *loquat* (page 197) is probably a

a. tree.
b. candy.
c. place.
d. fruit.

3. Why is Arnie bored on page 198?

a. He has finished all the loquats.
b. He thinks he's getting sunburned.
c. He isn't doing anything.
d. He doesn't have a book to read.

4. "José had already dropped his brushes on the side of the pool and hurried to the old man, who moaned, eyes closed, his false teeth jutting from his mouth." What is another way to say *jutting*?

a. showing under
b. sticking out
c. spilling over
d. sucking into

5. How did Mr. Clemens fall in the pool?

a. He was watching José work and he leaned over too far.
b. He was trying to find his hearing aid and tumbled in.
c. He bumped his head and lost his balance.
d. He jumped in after his poodle started barking too loudly.

6. Which excerpt from the story is an opinion?

a. " 'José's doing a good job,' Arnie said . . ."
b. "He gave the cleaned area a blast."
c. "He raised and lowered the back of the lounge."
d. " 'It's 940 East Brown . . .' "

7. Which happened first?

   a. Arnie rode away on his bike.
   b. Mr. Clemens started bleeding.
   c. José called 911.
   d. Mr. Clemens tried to stand up.

8. From the description on pages 200–201, you can infer that

   a. José is not really sure how he should act in this situation.
   b. José wishes he had followed Arnie and left Mr. Clemens there.
   c. José is trying to get help for Mr. Clemens as quickly as possible.
   d. José wants the poodle to sit down and stop barking.

9. Why does Arnie run away when Mr. Clemens falls?

   a. He is scared of Mr. Clemens.
   b. He doesn't want to finish the job.
   c. José tells him he should leave.
   d. He thinks they will be blamed.

10. Which character traits does José probably value most?

   a. friendliness and popularity
   b. maturity and a sense of humor
   c. stubbornness and intelligence
   d. honesty and hard work

Follow the Trail

Morals

A story often teaches us certain messages, lessons, or **morals**. Answer these questions about messages in "Born Worker, Part 2."

11. Authors sometimes reveal the messages of a story through its characters. They can do this by making certain characters more likable or appealing than others. How does the author use characters in "Born Worker" to reveal certain messages or lessons of the story?

    a. The author makes José the main character to show the value of hard, honest work.

    b. The author gives Arnie most of the dialogue to prove that good speaking ability is a strength.

    c. The author makes Mr. Clemens likable so that people will learn to take care of the elderly.

    d. The author uses all the characters to show that workers must be treated fairly.

12. How does the author use characters to criticize behavior in the story?

    a. The way that José refuses to speak to Arnie while he works teaches people that they should be polite at all times.

    b. Mr. Clemens's curiosity causes him to fall in the pool, so this shows that people should be more careful around the edge of a pool.

    c. Arnie's talking about vacations and being overly concerned with his new sneakers shows that spoiled children don't care about the important things in life.

    d. José's constant working is meant to show people that even if a person does a good job, he will not be rewarded.

13. What is one way that Arnie makes things difficult for José?

    a. He gives José detailed instructions about how to do his job.

    b. He criticizes José's work in front of Mr. Clemens.

    c. He distracts José by talking too much while José is trying to work.

    d. He doesn't share loquats with José.

14. On page 201, the author writes, "If he had been there, José's father would have seen that José was more than a good worker. He would have seen a good man." What do these lines show about the relationship between José and his father?

    a. José would do anything his father told him to do.
    b. José's father has been a good role model.
    c. They do not get along very well.
    d. José has a closer relationship with his mother.

15. What might be the final message the author is trying to send at the end of the story?

    a. Lying never gets anybody ahead.
    b. Cheating works as long as you don't get caught.
    c. Being a supervisor is better than being a worker.
    d. Good people take responsibility and help each other.

Find Word Meanings

The five words listed below appear in the second part of "Born Worker." Study the words and their definitions. Use the page numbers to check how the words are used in the story. Then complete the following sentences by using each vocabulary word only *once*.

word	meaning	page
babbled	chatted unintelligently, talked endlessly	198
stagnant	unmoving and dirty, stale	199
shuffling	walking with small steps, without lifting feet, dragging feet	199
buckled	folded, lost strength, gave way under	199
staggered	tripped over, walked unsteadily	200

    Once, I tried to do work outside on a really hot day. I wanted to plant some flowers to surprise my mom for her birthday. But working in the heat was harder than I thought. The air was thick and _____16_____ from the heat, humidity, and car fumes. It made it tough for me to breathe. After an hour of work, I didn't have the energy to move anymore; I was just dragging my feet and _____17_____ around. At one point, I felt so tired and

weak that my legs almost _____18_____ under me.
I _____19_____ inside the house to get a glass of cold water.
I drank it quickly and felt a lot better. Then I sat on the couch
and watched TV. As a guy on TV _____20_____ on and on
about something, I let myself drift off to sleep. I decided it was
better to take a little nap now, and finish the garden in the
evening when it was cooler outside!

Look at Language

Similes

As you learned, **similes** compare two unlike things using the
word *like* or *as* (for example, "His eyes are as blue as the ocean").
Answer these questions about similes in Part 2 of "Born Worker."

21. "José scrubbed. He worked the wire brush over the black
and green stains, the grime dripping like tears." What does
the simile "the grime dripping like tears" tell you about
José and his work?

 a. Arnie was being mean to José and making him cry.

 b. José was putting extreme physical and mental effort into
 his work.

 c. José was being a baby about all the tasks he had to
 accomplish.

 d. José was not getting the dirt to come off of the stains.

22. Which sentence about Mr. Clemens contains a simile?

 a. "He rolled once, and half of his body settled in the
 water."

 b. "His thin hair was combed so that his scalp, as pink as a
 crab, showed."

 c. "He was dressed in white pants and a flowery shirt."

 d. "He took shuffling steps toward the deep end."

23. "Then his hearing aid fell out, and José turned in time to see it roll like a bottle cap toward the bottom of the pool." What does the simile "roll like a bottle cap" help you understand?

    a. the small size of the hearing aid, and how it rolled away unevenly

    b. the fact that the hearing aid was a common and inexpensive item

    c. the fact that the hearing aid was a small and meaningless item

    d. the small size of the hearing aid, and how it smoothly glided across the floor

24. "He appeared startled, like a newborn." This simile tells you that after the accident, Mr. Clemens was

    a. helpless and childlike.

    b. upset with himself for being a baby.

    c. crying like an infant.

    d. feeling renewed and reborn.

25. "A fireman led José away and asked what had happened. He was starting to explain when his cousin reappeared, yapping like a poodle." The simile "yapping like a poodle" tells you that Arnie was

    a. calmly, intelligently telling the fireman what happened.

    b. speaking to the fireman in a loud, chatty, meaningless way.

    c. afraid to say much to the fireman.

    d. dancing around like a poodle as he talked.

Review the Case

The following activities will help you review and reflect on what happened in "Born Worker," Part 2.

1. **Discuss.** José does something interesting at the end of the story—he leaves Arnie talking to the paramedics and climbs up a telephone pole. Why do you think he does this? Explain. (You might want to look back at the beginning of the story on page 184.)

2. **Write.** Write two to three paragraphs comparing and contrasting the characters of Arnie and José. How are they alike and how are they different? How do these similarities and differences affect the events in the story?

3. **Technology Application.** Conduct research on first-aid procedures for common injuries, like cuts, scrapes, sprains, etc. Choose two injuries and write down step-by-step what you should do if someone gets injured in that way.

**The one thing of which I was fully conscious
was the awful heat that came up from
the dusty asphalt pavement as an
almost palpable wave.**

August Heat

by W. F. Harvey

PHENISTONE ROAD, CLAPHAM
August 20th, 190—

I have had what I believe to be the most remarkable day in my life, and while the events are still fresh in my mind, I wish to put them down on paper as clearly as possible.

Let me say at the outset that my name is James Clarence Withencroft.

I am forty years old, in perfect health, never having known a day's illness.

By profession I am an artist, not a very successful one, but I earn enough money by my black-and-white work to satisfy my necessary wants.

My only near relative, a sister, died five years ago, so that I am independent.

I breakfasted this morning at nine, and after glancing through the morning paper I lighted my pipe and proceeded to let my mind wander in the hope that I might chance upon some subject for my pencil.

The room, though door and windows were open, was oppressively hot, and I had just made up my mind that the coolest and most comfortable place in the neighborhood would be the deep end of the public swimming-bath, when the idea came.

I began to draw. So intent was I on my work that I left my lunch untouched, only stopping work when the clock of St. Jude's struck four.

The final result, for a hurried sketch, was, I felt sure, the best thing I had done.

It showed a criminal in the dock immediately after the judge had pronounced sentence. The man was fat—enormously fat. The flesh hung in rolls about his chin; it creased his huge, stumpy neck. He was clean-shaven (perhaps I should say a few days before he must have been clean shaven) and almost bald. He stood in the dock, his short, clumsy fingers clasping the rail, looking straight in front of him. The feeling that his expression conveyed was not so much one of horror as of utter, absolute collapse.

There seemed nothing in the man strong enough to sustain that mountain of flesh.

I rolled up the sketch, and without quite knowing why, placed it in my pocket. Then with the rare sense of happiness which the knowledge of a good thing well done gives, I left the house.

I believe that I set out with the idea of calling upon Trenton, for I remember walking along Lytton Street and turning to the right along Gilchrist Road at the bottom of the hill where the men were at work on the new tram lines.

From there onwards I have only the vaguest recollection of where I went. The one thing of which I was fully conscious was the awful heat, that came up from the dusty asphalt pavement as an almost palpable wave. I longed for the thunder promised by the great banks of copper-colored cloud that hung low over the western sky.

I must have walked five or six miles, when a small boy roused me from my reverie by asking the time.

It was twenty minutes to seven.

When he left me I began to take stock of my bearings. I found myself standing before a gate that led into a yard bordered by a strip of thirsty earth, where there were flowers, purple stock and scarlet geranium. Above the entrance was a board with the inscription:

CHS. ATKINSON
MONUMENTAL MASON
WORKER IN ENGLISH AND ITALIAN MARBLES

From the yard itself came a cheery whistle, the noise of hammer blows, and the cold sound of steel meeting stone.

A sudden impulse made me enter.

A man was sitting with his back towards me, busy at work on a slab of curiously veined marble. He turned round as he heard my steps and I stopped short.

It was the man I had been drawing, whose portrait lay in my pocket.

He sat there, huge and elephantine, the sweat pouring from his scalp, which he wiped with a red silk handkerchief. But though the face was the same, the expression was absolutely different.

He greeted me smiling, as if we were old friends, and shook my hand.

I apologized for my intrusion.

"Everything is hot and glary outside," I said. "This seems an oasis in the wilderness."

"I don't know about the oasis," he replied, "but it certainly is hot . . . Take a seat, sir!"

He pointed to the end of the gravestone on which he was at work, and I sat down.

"That's a beautiful piece of stone you've got hold of," I said.

He shook his head. "In a way it is," he answered; "the surface here is as fine as anything you could wish, but there's a big flaw at the back, though I don't expect you'd ever notice it. I could never make a really good job of a bit of marble like that. It would be all right in a summer like this; it wouldn't mind the blasted heat. But wait till the winter comes. There's nothing quite like frost to find out the weak points in stone."

"Then what's it for?" I asked.

The man burst out laughing.

"You'd hardly believe me if I was to tell you it's for an exhibition, but it's the truth. Artists have exhibitions: so do grocers and butchers; we have them too. All the latest little things in headstones, you know."

He went on to talk of marbles, which sort best withstood wind and rain, and which were easiest to work; then of his garden and a

new sort of carnation he had bought. At the end of every other minute he would drop his tools, wipe his shining head, and curse the heat.

I said little, for I felt uneasy. There was something unnatural, uncanny, in meeting this man.

I tried at first to persuade myself that I had seen him before, that his face, unknown to me, had found a place in some out-of-the-way corner of my memory, but I knew that I was practicing little more than a plausible piece of self-deception.

Mr. Atkinson finished his work, spat on the ground, and got up with a sigh of relief.

"There! What do you think of that?" he said, with an air of evident pride.

The inscription which I read for the first time was this:

SACRED TO THE MEMORY OF
JAMES CLARENCE WITHENCROFT
BORN JAN. 18TH, 1860
HE PASSED AWAY VERY SUDDENLY
ON AUGUST 20TH, 190—

"In the midst of life we are in death"

For some time I sat in silence. Then a cold shudder ran down my spine. I asked him where he had seen the name.

"Oh, I didn't see it anywhere," replied Mr. Atkinson. "I wanted some name, and I put down the first that came into my head. Why do you want to know?"

"It's a strange coincidence, but it happens to be mine."

He gave a long, low whistle.

"And the dates?"

"I can only answer for one of them, and that's correct."

"It's a rum go!" he said.

But he knew less than I did. I told him of my morning's work. I took the sketch from my pocket and showed it to him. As he looked, the expression of his face altered until it became more and more like that of the man I had drawn.

"And it was only the day before yesterday," he said, "that I told Maria there were no such things as ghosts!"

Neither of us had seen a ghost, but I knew what he meant.

"You probably heard my name," I said.

"And you must have seen me somewhere and have forgotten it! Were you at Clacton-on-Sea* last July?"

I had never been to Clacton in my life. We were silent for some time. We were both looking at the same thing, the two dates on the gravestone, and one was right.

"Come inside and have some supper," said Mr. Atkinson.

His wife is a cheerful little woman, with the flaky red cheeks of the country-bred. Her husband introduced me as a friend of his who was an artist. The result was unfortunate, for after the sardines and watercress had been removed, she brought out a Doré Bible, and I had to sit and express my admiration for nearly half an hour.

I went outside, and found Atkinson sitting on the gravestone smoking.

We resumed the conversation at the point we had left off.

"You must excuse my asking," I said, "but do you know of anything you've done for which you could be put on trial?"

He shook his head.

"I'm not a bankrupt, the business is prosperous enough. Three years ago I gave turkeys to some of the guardians at Christmas, but that's all I can think of. And they were small ones, too," he added as an afterthought.

He got up, fetched a can from the porch, and began to water the flowers. "Twice a day regular in the hot weather," he said, "and

---

*Clacton-on-Sea: a seaside resort in England

then the heat sometimes gets the better of the delicate ones. And ferns, good Lord! They could never stand it. Where do you live?"

I told him my address. It would take an hour's quick walk to get back home.

"It's like this," he said. "We'll look at the matter straight. If you go back home tonight, you take your chance of accidents. A cart may run over you, and there's always banana skins and orange peel, to say nothing of falling ladders."

He spoke of the improbable with an intense seriousness that would have been laughable six hours before. But I did not laugh.

"The best thing we can do," he continued, "is for you to stay here till twelve o'clock. We'll go upstairs and smoke; it may be cooler inside."

To my surprise I agreed.

◆

We are sitting now in a long, low room beneath the eaves. Atkinson has sent his wife to bed. He himself is busy sharpening some tools at a little oilstone, smoking one of my cigars the while.

The air seems charged with thunder. I am writing this at a shaky table before the open window. The leg is cracked, and Atkinson, who seems a handy man with his tools, is going to mend it as soon as he has finished putting an edge on his chisel.

It is after eleven now. I shall be gone in less than an hour.

But the heat is stifling.

It is enough to send a man mad.

Now it's time for YOU to be the Reader as Detective.

"August Heat" seems to end at this point. But the story actually continues—in your imagination. What do you think will happen *now*? Think back to the drawing and the gravestone. Read the last four paragraphs of the story again. What is going to happen, Reader as Detective?

Be a Reading Detective

Read each of the following questions. Then write the letter of the correct answer to each question. Remember, the symbol next to each question identifies the *kind* of reading skill that particular question helps you to develop.

1. James Clarence Withencroft was
   a. an artist.
   b. a stonecutter.
   c. a famous writer.
   d. a ghost.

2. Which group of words BEST describes the man in the drawing?
   a. clean shaven, thin, nearly bald
   b. clean shaven, fat, tired
   c. thick neck, clumsy fingers, heavy beard
   d. hairy, barrel chested, sweaty

3. You can infer that
   a. Withencroft returned home after twelve o'clock.
   b. Withencroft had an accident on his way home.
   c. Atkinson killed Withencroft.
   d. Atkinson protected Withencroft.

4. This story takes place
   a. on a hot day in August.
   b. on January 18, 1860.
   c. at Clacton in July.
   d. the day after a trial.

5. Which one of the following happened after Atkinson and Withencroft ate supper?
   a. Withencroft walked along Lytton Street and then up Gilchrist Road.
   b. Atkinson discussed different kinds of marble.
   c. Withencroft went upstairs to relax.
   d. Mrs. Atkinson prepared for bed.

6. Withencroft completed "a hurried sketch." Which of the following BEST defines the word *sketch*?
   a. rough drawing
   b. headstone
   c. artist's show
   d. quick poem

7. Which of the following describes Atkinson?
   a. He didn't mind the heat.
   b. He was not very handy.
   c. He looked like the man in the picture.
   d. He was quite slender.

8. Which statement expresses an opinion?
   a. "The final result, for a hurried sketch, was, I felt sure, the best thing I had done."
   b. "He got up, fetched a can from the porch, and began to water the flowers."
   c. "I am writing this at a shaky table before the open window."
   d. "I had never been to Clacton in my life."

9. Atkinson was busy putting "an edge on his chisel." Which expression BEST defines the word *chisel* as used in this sentence?
   a. cheat or trick
   b. cut out or shape
   c. sharp tool
   d. small hammer

10. This story is mainly about
    a. how a man takes a long walk on a very hot day.
    b. how strange events suggest that a man will be killed.
    c. the way to make headstones.
    d. the way artists make a living.

Follow the Trail

Conclusions

You are aware that a good reader uses facts and story clues to **draw conclusions**. Few stories offer the reader more opportunities to practice this skill than "August Heat." It is truly a story that demands that the reader be a reading detective.

Answer each of the questions below. Think carefully about what happens in the story as you draw your conclusions.

11. You can conclude that Atkinson
    a. fixed the table and went straight to bed.
    b. helped Withencroft arrive home safely.
    c. killed Withencroft some time before midnight.
    d. turned Withencroft out of his house.

12. Probably, Atkinson was greatly affected by
    a. the fear that Withencroft would murder him.
    b. the unbearable heat, which drove him mad.
    c. jealousy over Withencroft's wealth.
    d. discomfort over his own artistic ability.

13. Evidence in the story leads us to guess that Withencroft was killed by
    a. a sharp chisel.
    b. a heavy stone.
    c. a bad fall.
    d. poisoned food.

14. The picture that Withencroft drew suggests that
    a. he had never been in a courthouse.
    b. his murderer was caught and sentenced.
    c. Atkinson was never seen or heard from again.
    d. he was not a very good artist.

15. There is reason to conclude that Withencroft
    a. was planning to become a stonecutter.
    b. later sold his paintings for much money.
    c. died on August 20.
    d. had a weak imagination.

Find Word Meanings

The five words listed below appear in "August Heat." Study the words and their definitions. Use the page numbers to check how the words are used in the story. Then complete the following sentences by using each vocabulary word only *once*.

word	meaning	page
remarkable	unusual	209
intent	strong purpose; strongly fixed on something	210
conveyed	expressed or communicated	210
vaguest	slightest; very unclear	210
coincidence	the chance happening of two things in such a way as to be striking or unusual	213

"August Heat" is one of the most _____16_____ stories ever written. If you read it too quickly, you will have only the _____17_____ idea of what happened. But if you read it more carefully, you will be able to understand what the author has _____18_____. By paying close attention to details, you will be able to comprehend the meaning behind each striking or unusual _____19_____ in the story, and you will develop an understanding of the author's purpose, or _____20_____.

Look at Language

Context Clues

Often, you can figure out the meaning of a difficult or unfamiliar word by looking at the *context*—the words (and sometimes the sentences) around the word. **Context clues** will help you find the word's meaning.

As the Reader as Detective, you have already had experience using vocabulary clues to figure out word meanings. The following questions will provide additional practice using context clues to find the word's meaning.

21. "I breakfasted this morning at nine, and after glancing through the morning paper I lighted my pipe and proceeded to let my mind wander in the hope that I might chance upon some subject for my pencil." *Proceeded* means

    a. went on to.
    b. marched.
    c. prevented.
    d. attempted.

22. When the narrator says that he apologized for his "intrusion" (page 211), he is apologizing for

    a. entering uninvited.
    b. criticizing the man's yard.
    c. making too much noise.
    d. breaking in.

23. " 'Everything is hot and glary outside,' I said. 'This seems an *oasis* in the wilderness.' " An *oasis* is a

    a. place that provides relief.
    b. hot and sticky place.
    c. swimming pool.
    d. hidden trap.

24. "As he looked, the expression of his face altered until it became more and more like that of the man I had drawn." *Altered* means

    a. grew larger.
    b. angered.
    c. changed.
    d. disappeared.

25. " 'I'm not a bankrupt, the business is prosperous enough.' " *Prosperous* means

    a. secretive.
    b. well known.
    c. growing and successful.
    d. suffering.

Review the Case

The following activities will help you review and reflect on what happened in "August Heat."

1. Discuss. How do you think it's possible that Withencroft and Atkinson know of each other? Or is that just a device the author used to write a mysterious story?

2. Write. Explain how each of the following played an important part in "August Heat." Answer in a few sentences for each.

> **A.** The picture that Withencroft drew
>
> **B.** The gravestone that Atkinson made
>
> **C.** The terrible heat

Later, you and your classmates can share ideas about what happened to Withencroft.

3. Technology Application. Use your home, school, or library computer to create an advertisement for Charles Atkinson's business. It could appear in a magazine, on a billboard, or as a flyer. Make sure you use visuals and give all the pertinent information customers would need to contact Atkinson.

He looked down at me with something like scorn. "Be brave, little fellow. Die like a soldier!"

Every Fifth Man

by Edward D. Hoch

You probably wonder why I'm still alive after all that has happened, and I suppose it is quite a story. I'd been living and training with the exiles for two years before the attempted coup, knowing—as we all knew—the penalty for failure. There were months of hand-to-hand combat and paratrooper training and even some explosives practice before we were ready for the big day, the day we returned to Costanera.

I'd lived the 25 years of my life in the cities and towns and jungle villages of Costanera. It was my country, worth fighting for, every inch of it. We left with the coming of General Diam, but now we were going back. We would drop from the skies by night, join the anti-Diam military, and enter the capital city in triumph.

That was the plan. Somehow it didn't work out that way. The military changed their minds about it, and we jumped

from our planes into a withering crossfire from General Diam's forces. More than half of our liberation force of 65 were dead before we reached the ground, and the others were overrun quickly. By nightfall we found ourselves prisoners of the army in the great old fortress overlooking Azul Bay.

There were 23 of us taken prisoner that day, and of these one man—Tomas—had a bad wound in his side. We were crowded into a single large cell at the fortress and left to await our fate. It was hot in there, with the sweat of bodies and a mustiness of air that caught at my throat and threatened to choke me. I wanted to remove my black beret and shirt and stretch out on the hard stone floor, but I did not. Instead I bore it in silence and waited with the others.

A certain custom has existed in the country, a custom which has been observed in revolutions for hundreds of years. Always faced with the problem of the defeated foe, governments had traditionally sent down the order. *Kill every fifth man and release the others.* It was a system of justice tempered with a large degree of mercy, and acted as a deterrent while still allowing something of an opposition party to exist within the country. Of course the eighty percent who were released often regrouped to revolt again, but the threat that hung over them was sometimes enough to pacify their activities.

This, then, was the fate that awaited us—23 prisoners in a gloomy fortress by the blue waters of a bay. We had reason to hope, because most of us had the odds on our side, but we had reckoned without the cold-blooded calculation of General Diam. The order came down early the following morning, and it was read to us through the bars of the cell. It was as we had expected: *Every fifth man will be executed immediately. The remaining prisoners will be released in twenty-four hours.*

But then came the jolting surprise. The officer in charge kept reading, and read the same message four times more. General Diam had sent down five identical executive orders. No one was to survive the executions.

I knew something had to be done, and quickly. As the guards unlocked the cell door I went to the officer in charge. Using my deepest voice I tried to reason with him. "You cannot execute all twenty-three of us. It would be contrary to orders."

He looked down at me with something like scorn. "Be brave, little fellow. Die like a soldier!"

"But the first order says that every fifth man should be executed immediately. It means just that. They should be executed before you read the second order."

The officer sighed. "What difference does it make? The day will be hot. Who wants to die under the noonday sun? At least now there is a bit of breeze out there."

"You must obey the orders," I insisted. "Each order must be executed separately."

You can see, of course, the reason for my insistence. If the five executive orders were lumped together and carried out at once (as General Diam no doubt intended), all twenty-three of us would be shot. But if they were carried out separately, the orders would allow nine of us to live. I'd always been good at mathematics, and this was how I figured it—every fifth man would be taken from the original 23, a total of 4, leaving 19. The process would be repeated a second time, killing 3, leaving 16. On the third round another 3 would die, and 13 would be left. Then 2 shot, 11 left. A final 2 shot, and 9 of us would walk out of the fortress as free as the air.

You say the odds were still against me? Not at all—if the officer agreed to my argument, I was certain to survive. Because consider—how would the fifth man be picked each time? Not by drawing straws, for this was the military. We would line up in a single column and count off. And in what order would we line up—alphabetically? Hardly, when they did not even know our names. We would line up in the old military tradition—by height.

And I had already established during the night in the cell that I was the shortest of the 23 prisoners!

If they started the count-off at the short end of the line—which was unlikely—I would always be safe, for I would always be Number One. More likely, they would start at the tall end, and for the 5 count-offs I would always be last —numbers 23, 19, 16, 13,

11, and 9. Never a number divisible by 5—never one of the doomed prisoners!

The officer stared down at me for what seemed an eternity. Finally he glanced through the orders in his hand once more and reached a decision.

"All right, we will carry out the first order."

We lined up in the courtyard—by height—with two men supporting the wounded Tomas, and started the count-off. Of the 23 of us, 4 were marched over to the sea wall and shot. The rest of us tried not to look.

Again—and 3 of our number died against the sea wall. One of the remaining 16 started to cry. He had figured out his position in the line.

The officer formally read the third executive order, and 3 more went to the wall. I was still last in the line.

After the fourth order 2 of the 13 were marched to their death. Even the firing squad was beginning to look hot and bored. The sun was almost above us. Well, only one more count-off and then 9 of us would be free.

"Wait!" the officer shouted, as the first man began to count off again. I turned my neck in horror. Tomas had fallen from the line and the blood was gushing from his side. He was dead, and the 11 suddenly reduced to 10. I was the tenth one as the last count began!

The fifth man stepped out of line—then *six, seven, eight, nine, ten*. I didn't move.

"Come, little fellow," the officer said. "It is your turn now."

You ask how I come to be sitting here, when I was so surely doomed, when my careful figuring had gone for nothing. I stood there in that moment, looking death in the face, and did what I had kept from doing all night and morning. I knew the officer would obey General Diam's order to the letter—to execute every fifth man—and that was what saved me.

Now it's time for YOU to be the Reader as Detective.

 You know the author survived to tell the story. Knowing what you know up to this point, how do you think the author managed to escape? Finish the story to see how it happens.

I took the beret from my head, let my hair fall to my shoulders, and showed them I was a girl.

Be a Reading Detective

Read each of the following questions. Then write the letter of the correct answer to each question. Remember, the symbol next to each question identifies the *kind* of reading skill that particular question helps you to develop.

1. From the information given at the beginning of the story, what do you think the *liberation force* is on page 222?
   a. a poorly organized army
   b. a group fighting for freedom
   c. people who are taken prisoner
   d. people who are sentenced to death

2. Which opinion is the reason the narrator is a soldier?
   a. She wants other people to think she's tough.
   b. She believes her country is worth fighting for.
   c. She has great respect for General Diam.
   d. She is very good at doing math.

3. According to the information on page 222, what is the main reason leaders usually kill every fifth man and let others go?
   a. The leaders want people to know they have mercy.
   b. The government is simply following the custom.
   c. The survivors might be too scared to try anything again.
   d. The government doesn't want to kill too many people.

4. "Of course the eighty percent who were released often regrouped to revolt again, but the threat that hung over them was sometimes enough to pacify their activities." In this sentence, "pacify their activities" means to

a. ease or stop their fighting.
b. energize their fighting.
c. strengthen their fighting.
d. disapprove of their fighting.

5. We first find out the narrator survives

a. in the final paragraph.
b. in the very beginning of the story.
c. during the shootings at the sea wall.
d. when the group is first taken prisoner.

6. Why does the guard call the narrator "little fellow" on pages 222 and 224?

a. He thinks she should be shot.
b. He is trying to be nice.
c. He is making fun of her.
d. She is smaller than the others.

7. What happened immediately after the guard agreed to execute each order separately?

a. The first four prisoners were shot.
b. Tomas died from his wounds.
c. The guards counted the prisoners.
d. The prisoners were lined up by height.

8. Which is an important fact in the story?

a. The narrator is sneaky.
b. The narrator is not very brave.
c. The officer is too easily persuaded.
d. The narrator is a girl.

9. On page 224, why does one of the prisoners start to cry?

a. He is afraid because he sees his friends dying.
b. He has been wounded and he is in pain.

c. He knows he will be shot in the next round.

d. He is nervous that he will not survive all the rounds.

10. According to the information on page 222, General Diam most likely intended that

a. all the prisoners be shot.

b. only the male prisoners be shot.

c. each order should be carried out separately.

d. nine prisoners should be set free.

Follow the Trail

Setting

The **setting** of a story is the time and place in which a story occurs. A story may take place at the seaside in the seventeenth century, or in an imaginary kingdom some time long ago, or in a different galaxy thousands of years in the future.

Just as a detective thinks about the setting of a crime, the reader must think about the setting of a story. When and where a story takes place influence the characters, events, and ideas in that story. Answer the following questions about the setting of "Every Fifth Man."

11. When are General Diam's orders carried out?

a. the night after the prisoners are taken in

b. 25 years after the prisoners are taken in

c. the morning after the prisoners are taken in

d. two years after the prisoners are taken in

12. The heat and discomfort of the jail cell

a. reflect the anxiety the prisoners are feeling.

b. show that the ruling party is cruel to prisoners.

c. help the narrator to stay standing, wearing her hat.

d. are signs that the story takes place in summer.

13. Why do the officers want to execute the orders as quickly as possible?

    a. They do not want to cross General Diam.

    b. They are tired of taking care of the prisoners.

    c. The prison cell is needed for another purpose.

    d. It is going to get very hot very soon.

14. According to the story, how is the sea different from the fortress and the prisoners?

    a. The sea is a violent, crashing force, but the fortress is stable because the prisoners are controlled.

    b. The sea water is calm and blue, but in the fortress, there is chaos among the prisoners.

    c. The sea is beautiful, blue, and free, while the fortress and prisoners are gray and sad.

    d. The sea is warm and inviting, whereas the fortress is cold and scary for the prisoners.

15. The final paragraph of the story takes place

    a. outside, by the sea wall.

    b. in the jungle.

    c. in the prison.

    d. on the beach.

Find Word Meanings

The five words listed below appear in "Every Fifth Man." Study the words and their definitions. Use the page numbers to check how the words are used in the story. Then complete the following sentences by using each vocabulary word only *once*.

word	meaning	page
paratrooper	a soldier who parachutes into enemy territory	221
withering	attempting to cut down	222
mustiness	stuffiness, moldiness	222
tempered	made less intense, toned down	222
deterrent	something that discourages somebody from doing something	222

When the _____16_____ landed, he quickly rolled up his parachute. The swamp's smell of _____17_____ was overwhelming as he waded through the knee-deep water. A hot sun did not help to keep up his _____18_____ strength. Although his fear was a serious _____19_____, he knew he would have to take a rest. He _____20_____ his anxiety by climbing into a tree, where he thought he would be harder to spot.

Look at Language

Descriptive Language

Remember that writers use vivid, **descriptive language** to bring a story alive for readers.

Answer the following questions about descriptive language in "Every Fifth Man."

21. "A final 2 shot, and 9 of us would walk out of the fortress as free as the air." This is a descriptive way of showing that the nine prisoners would
    a. be given the chance to walk around while they wait.
    b. be released from prison and given their freedom.
    c. have their spirits ascend into the air.
    d. sneak out of the prison to gain freedom.

22. "Instead I bore it in silence and waited with the others." This shows you that the narrator is
    a. strong and fights to overcome physical fatigue.
    b. too shy to express her real feelings.
    c. too modest to change into more comfortable clothes.
    d. not brave enough to take any real action.

23. Why would the narrator say "The officer stared down at me for what seemed an eternity"?
    a. This shows just how short the narrator actually is.
    b. The writer is trying to show that the situation is confusing.
    c. The officer seems to be very strict and scary.
    d. Making the time go more slowly builds suspense.

24. "It was my country, worth fighting for, every inch of it."
The narrator means that she
   a. won't rest until she has visited every inch of her country.
   b. has lived in different parts of the country and feels loyal to all of it.
   c. is going to fight battles on every inch of soil in her country.
   d. owns a great deal of valuable land.

25. "I stood there in that moment, looking death in the face, and did what I had kept from doing all night and morning." The phrase "looking death in the face" tells us that she
   a. bravely faces the fact that she might be about to die.
   b. gives in and accepts that she will die.
   c. has been shot and is about to die.
   d. is dead and can see her afterlife.

Review the Case

The following activities will help you review and reflect on what happened in "Every Fifth Man."

1. **Discuss.** Do you believe the country where you were born is worth fighting for? Why or why not?

2. **Write.** Imagine the narrator as she was when she was a child growing up in Costanera. Write a description of a typical, happy day in the narrator's childhood.

3. **Technology Application.** Revolutions, violent or nonviolent, have occurred in many countries around the world. Using electronic research sources, find out the details of one such revolution and prepare a list of bullet points to summarize where the revolution occurred, why it occurred, how it occurred, and what happened as a result.

Snow hoped to solve the mystery once and for all, but first he needed ammunition: papers and reports about the outlaws' physical characteristics and medical condition.

On the Outlaw Trail

by Peggy Thomas

Clyde Snow enjoys going after the bad guys, especially when they are already dead. When he was presented with the mystery of Robert Leroy Parker and Harry A. Longabaugh, better known as Butch Cassidy and the Sundance Kid, he was excited to join the chase.

Butch and Sundance were two of the most notorious, elusive, and romanticized outlaws of the Wild West, staying one step ahead of the law before finally fleeing to South America in the early 1900s. From there the story gets muddled and mythical. Did they settle down and become cattle ranchers in Bolivia or did they come back to the United States as some stories claim? Were they buried in a remote village in Bolivia after being gunned down by Bolivian army soldiers? Snow hoped to solve the mystery once and for

all, but first he needed ammunition: papers and reports about the outlaws' physical characteristics and medical condition. Snow found what he was looking for in old prison records and Pinkerton detective reports. Armed with this information, Snow and a team of historians, archaeologists, and forensic researchers set off for the dusty mining town in San Vicente, Bolivia.

San Vicente lies 15,000 feet above sea level high in the Andes. Snow described the landscape as so sparse the buzzards had to pack a lunch. On the outskirts of town, surrounded by a tall mud-brick wall was a cemetery. Inside the wall was a sea of tombstones and wooden crosses; new graves mingled with the old. In the middle of the maze, under a small block of stone that had long since lost its plaque and cross, the two outlaws were said to have been buried.

Butch and Sundance's last heist was robbing a courier carrying a mining company's payroll. The courier collected three Bolivian army soldiers who tracked the outlaws to San Vicente where they had rented a room for the night. As the soldiers approached the sun-dried brick house, they saw Butch and Sundance's rifles leaning against the wall by the door. The soldiers ordered the outlaws to come out. The records are confused as to who shot first, but the official record from the Bolivian army states that the two men ran out into the courtyard where the shorter outlaw (Butch) shot the other in the forehead and then turned the gun on himself, committing suicide. The two were buried in the village cemetery.

Two tall European-looking North Americans in a cemetery full of shorter, more compact South Americans should be easy to pick out, but Snow and his team discovered a problem. A Swedish miner, who shot himself accidentally while trying to get down off his mule, and a German prospector, who blew himself up while thawing frozen dynamite in an oven, were also buried somewhere in the cemetery. There would be a chance of digging them up instead of the outlaws.

Now it's time for YOU to be the Reader as Detective.

What do you think will happen when investigators open the graves? Will they find the two notorious outlaws? Read on to find out!

The exhumation began after a local shaman gave an offering to appease the spirits for disturbing the grave site. The first bones found were loose stray bones from older graves that had been moved to make room for newer ones, a common practice where space is limited. Digging further, they found what they were looking for, a complete skeleton. The coffin had disintegrated leaving only stray nails every few inches. They found buttons similar to those on a denim jacket and a belt buckle. The skull was lifted out for Snow to inspect. He turned it in his hands and declared it to be a Caucasian male. The mandible[1] was hoisted up next. From the teeth, Snow estimated the age between 30 and 40 years old. Snow had seen so many bones that a quick look was enough to tell him that they were on the right track. "Like anything else, the more you do a job the better you get," he said.

After two days of digging, only one skeleton was uncovered. The remains were taken back to the United States where a team of experts, a microscopist, forensic odontologist,[2] podiatrist, and radiologist would add to the story. An anthropologist seldom works alone. The most thorough investigation requires a multi-disciplinary approach.

The microscopist examined the buttons and belt buckles for any identifying marks or inscriptions. They were made in the United States at the turn of the [20th] century. The radiologist X-rayed the bones, looking for metal fragments from bullet wounds and traces of healed broken bones.

The scientists met to pool their research, listing their discoveries on a chalk board. Was the skeleton found in the San Vicente grave Butch? No, the skeleton was too tall for it to be Butch, and a superimposition of the skull with a photograph taken of Butch at the Wyoming prison in 1894 did not correspond at all.

Their hopes were pinned on Sundance. The skull's head injury corresponded with the written reports of Sundance having been shot in the head, but the damage to the skull made it difficult to superimpose the skull with a photograph. Some of the reference points lined up, but not enough of the skull was present to make identification conclusive. In forensics there is no room for reasonable doubt.

---

[1]mandible: jaw.

[2]forensic odontologist: a scientist that handles dental evidence.

The Pinkerton Agency

The Pinkerton Agency was founded by Allan Pinkerton in 1850. It soon became one of the most important crime detection and law enforcement groups in the United States.

While working as a barrel maker outside of Chicago, Pinkerton suspected he knew the hideout of a band of counterfeiters. He alerted the local sheriff and the two staked out the area, which led to the arrest of the band, minus the ringleader.

Pinkerton's help in tracking down the leader led to Pinkerton's being appointed a deputy sheriff for Kane County. In 1850, he became Chicago's first police detective. With attorney Edward Rucker, Pinkerton founded the North-Western Police Agency.

In 1843, Allan's brother, Robert, started his own railroad contracting business but later became a railroad detective. He had many contracts with Wells Fargo to supply stagecoaches with guards and, afterward, with railroad and stagecoach detectives.

Eventually Allan joined Robert in what became the Pinkerton National Detective Agency. Among the detective services they provided was capturing counterfeiters and train robbers.

In 1861, the Pinkerton Agency revealed an assassination plot against Abraham Lincoln. Conspirators had plotted to kill Lincoln in Baltimore, on the way to his inauguration. Thanks to Pinkerton's warning, Lincoln changed his plans and, during the Civil War, he used the Pinkerton Agency in a variety of ways. A "secret service" was organized. Pinkerton agents secured military information on the Confederates and some acted as Lincoln's bodyguards.

After the war ended, the government often used the Pinkerton Agency to perform many of the duties of the present-day Secret Service, CIA, and FBI. Since the agency also worked for the railroads and overland stage companies, it pursued many outlaws, including Butch Cassidy and his Wild Bunch.

On the Chicago building that housed the Pinkerton Agency was the Agency's logo: a black-and-white eye with the legendary motto "We Never Sleep."

This agency was the original "private eye."

A podiatrist looked at the leg and foot bones and the remains of the shoes. He discovered that the person would have walked with an unusual gait, because of the angle of the bones. The historian pointed out that Sundance had another nickname, "the Straddler," because he walked bowlegged and with a limp. Snow wondered if this condition was hereditary and tracked down Sundance's distant relatives, the Longabaughs, in Pennsylvania. The males in the family all walked slightly bowlegged because of the way their toes curled up. That was one piece of evidence that strongly suggested the skeleton was Sundance.

The radiologist showed the other scientists the X-rays that revealed some shrapnel in the cranium that would be consistent with a bullet in the head, but there was no sign of a healed gunshot wound that Sundance was reported to have had.

The last step in identifying the skeleton was to try to match samples of DNA from the bones, with samples of DNA from Sundance's nearest blood relative, a member of the Longabaugh family. The DNA did not match. Whoever the man in the cemetery was it was neither Butch nor Sundance.

Be a Reading Detective

Read each of the following questions. Then write the letter of the correct answer to each question. Remember, the symbol next to each question identifies the *kind* of reading skill that particular question helps you to develop.

1. This selection is mainly about
   a. figuring out what happened to Butch Cassidy and the Sundance Kid.
   b. exactly what is involved in being an anthropologist.
   c. the history of robbers in the Wild West.
   d. how bodies can be exhumed for examination.

2. Why would Butch's and the Sundance Kid's remains have been easy to identify in the graveyard?

a. They would have been larger than other bodies buried there.
b. They would have been smaller than other bodies buried there.
c. They each would have had bullet holes all over their bodies.
d. They each had unique dental records.

3. Based on the use of the word *mingled* in the third paragraph, to *mingle* most likely means

a. to deceive.
b. to approach.
c. to overwhelm.
d. to mix.

4. Based on the information on page 235, what is a *podiatrist*?

a. a DNA scientist
b. a person who studies X-rays
c. a foot doctor
d. a historian

5. Which of these happened first?

a. Authorities used dental records to try identify the remains.
b. A shaman gave an offering to appease the spirits.
c. The bodies in San Vicente were exhumed.
d. Stray bones were found in the top of the grave.

6. Which was *not* a fact in Clyde Snow's file?

a. The Sundance Kid had relatives who could be contacted.
b. Three Bolivian soldiers tracked the robbers after a heist.
c. The buttons and belt buckles in the grave were made in the United States.
d. The fate of Butch and Sundance would be difficult to determine.

7. "... a team of experts, a microscopist, forensic odontologist, podiatrist, and radiologist would add to the story. An anthropologist seldom works alone. The most thorough investigation requires a multidisciplinary approach." Based on the context, *multidisciplinary* means

   a. involving more than one anthropologist at a time.
   b. involving more than one field of study.
   c. requiring hard work and discipline.
   d. involving many steps of research.

8. The main idea of the third paragraph is

   a. Butch and Sundance were buried in San Vicente.
   b. San Vicente is located in the Andes.
   c. San Vicente is a lonely, desolate town.
   d. There are very old buildings in San Vicente.

9. What can you infer about the courier in the fourth paragraph?

   a. He called for help because he was a coward.
   b. He knew exactly where the robbers were hiding.
   c. He survived Butch and Sundance's robbery.
   d. He helped Butch and Sundance steal the payroll money.

10. How did scientists decide the skull did not belong to Butch?

   a. The skull did not show signs that its owner had been shot in the head.
   b. The skull clearly belonged to a man older than Butch was at the time of his death.
   c. The skull showed that the body would have been taller than Butch was.
   d. It did not match prison photographs taken of him at the time.

Follow the Trail

Text Structure

When an author writes something, whether it's a poem, a story, or an informational article like the one you just read, the author makes choices about how to structure the writing. Sometimes authors organize writing using **chronological order** (or **time order**), the order in which events actually did or would actually happen. Authors also use a **problem-solution order,** where a problem is given and then a solution or solutions are discussed. They also use **cause and effect,** where one event leads to or causes another.

Authors might also use **text features** to set apart important or additional information. These include bulleted lists, footnotes, sidebars, illustrations, and headings.

Look carefully at the structure of "On the Outlaw Trail" and then answer the following questions.

11. In the second paragraph, the author uses _____ to build interest in the topic of the article.

   a. historical information
   b. DNA evidence
   c. questions
   d. legends

12. According to the sidebar, the name "Pinkerton" comes from

   a. the color of the agency's logo.
   b. the place where the agency started.
   c. the bank where the agency had an account.
   d. the name of the agency's founder.

13. The sidebar is organized mostly through

   a. spatial order.
   b. chronological order.
   c. cause and effect.
   d. problem and solution.

14. What text feature would *not* be appropriate to add to this article?

   a. a diagram of DNA
   b. a photograph of the outlaws

    c. a chart listing other outlaws from the same time
    d. a map of the area where the outlaws were last seen

15. According to the sidebar, the primary purpose of the Pinkerton agency was

    a. transportation.
    b. detective work.
    c. banking.
    d. construction.

Find Word Meanings

The five words listed below appear in "On the Outlaw Trail." Study the words and their definitions. Use the page numbers to check how the words are used in the story. Then complete the following sentences by using each vocabulary word only *once*.

word	meaning	page
romanticized	made to seem larger than life, or more fanciful	231
ammunition	items that are used in attacking or defending something or someone	232
sparse	not dense, thinly populated, bare	232
exhumation	removal of a body from a grave for examination	233
disintegrated	fell apart, broke down	233

    Police wanted to know what kind of _____16_____ had been used in the shooting murder. The bullets were still in the buried body, so they would have to do an _____17_____ to get them. Because the coffin had been in the ground for so long, it _____18_____ as the crane lifted it out.

    The evidence left to the police was _____19_____. This was definitely not a case that would be _____20_____ on a television crime series.

Look at Language

Context Clues

Often, you can figure out the meaning of a difficult or unfamiliar word by looking at the *context*—the words (and sometimes the sentences) around the word. **Context clues** will help you find the word's meaning.

As the Reader as Detective, you have already had experience in using vocabulary clues to figure out word meanings. The following questions will provide additional practice in using context clues to find the word's meaning.

21. "The scientists met to pool their research, listing their discoveries on a chalk board." *Pool* means

   a. put together.
   b. bet on.
   c. prove.
   d. vote on.

22. "The skull's head injury corresponded with the written reports of Sundance having been shot in the head, but the damage to the skull made it difficult to *superimpose* the skull with a photograph." *Superimpose* means to

   a. replace one thing with something else.
   b. put one thing on top of another.
   c. set two things side by side.
   d. see clearly.

23. "Some of the reference points lined up, but not enough of the skull was present to make identification conclusive. In forensics there is no room for reasonable doubt." *Conclusive* means

   a. definite, without a doubt.
   b. tentative and awaiting proof.
   c. full of clues and hints.
   d. easy to determine.

24. "Snow wondered if this condition was hereditary and tracked down Sundance's distant relatives, the Longabaughs, in Pennsylvania." *Hereditary* means

a. contagious.
b. avoidable.
c. passed down through families.
d. specific to Pennsylvania.

25. "Since the agency also worked for the railroads and overland stage companies, it pursued many outlaws, including Butch Cassidy and his Wild Bunch." *Pursued* means

a. arrested.
b. went after.
c. found.
d. assisted.

Review the Case

The following activities will help you review and reflect on what happened in "On the Outlaw Trail."

1. **Discuss.** How does the information in the sidebar on page 234 contribute to the article as a whole?

2. **Write.** Write a two-paragraph diary entry for either one of the outlaws while they were on the run, or Clyde Snow as he was trying to find out their fate.

3. **Technology Application.** Find out more about Butch Cassidy and the Sundance Kid. Conduct research and create a time line of the criminals' careers with the information you find.

The Grind of an Axe

PART I

by Theodore Taylor

The call from a girl who said she was Gudrid Karlsevne, from the island of Bornholm, off Sweden, came through about three thirty in the afternoon, California time. She said she was answering the ad in the Stockholm newspaper for a nursemaid. She was the first of several girls named Karlsevne who answered it.

I knew that my father, Snorre Karlsevne, had placed such an ad. My mother was a career woman in stocks and bonds and intended to return to work after giving birth.

"Neither my mother or father are here," I said.

I told Gudrid, who spoke English with a soft accent and sounded very nice, that I was their daughter, Wendy, and would have my mother call her back. Mother was at the doctor's office, the baby due in a month. My father, who worked for Cal-Aero, was in Saudi Arabia, expected home within two weeks, in time for the estimated arrival of my new brother or sister.

"Have you ever been to America?" I asked.

"No, but I hope I can come over and take care of the new child."

I asked how old she was.

"Twenty."

Since I was sixteen, I thought it might be fun to be around her. She was probably tall, blond, and beautiful and could tell me all sorts of things about Scandinavia. I promised I'd have my mother call her back the minute she returned.

In the ad, my father has requested that the nursemaid be named Karlsevne. Let me explain: My father is a Vikingperson just like there are American Irishpersons and Britishpersons and Frenchpersons and Dutchpersons, who often make bores out of themselves talking about the *auld sod*, Trafalgar Square, Paris, and Rotterdam.

My father would proudly tell anyone that Torfinn Karlsevne was the first man to discover America, 488 years before Columbus. I once made the mistake of showing him an article that said Leif Ericsson reached either Newfoundland or Nova Scotia in A.D. 999. Either way, Norwegians discovered America.

Jaw set, blue eyes impaling me, he said, "Thorfinn, or Torfinn, and his wife had a son named Snorre, and that's eventually how I got my name. It all happened at Hudson Bay." Then he showed me a book that said the same thing. According to the family tree, my father was the seventy-eighth Snorre Karlsevne.

My mother, Harriet, got home from the doctor about twenty minutes later and I told her about the call from Bornholm. She laughed and shook her head. "Gudrid is the first name of your father's great-great grandmother. He'll be pleased. What a family!" She always tended to laugh about the Viking thing. She was a farm girl from Kansas and demanded good English names for her children. Hence, Wendy is my name.

She called Bornholm a few minutes later and talked with Gudrid for a long time, finally asking for her personal recommendations and phone numbers from people in Sweden who could speak English. We received a fax within an hour and within a few days she got the job. A date was set for her to arrive in San Francisco in two weeks.

After that conversation, a strange thing happened. Looking back, it all seemed so innocent but it brought us to the brink of terror. Operator 651, in San Francisco, called to say she had a cablegram from Sweden addressed to my father. The operator read it while Mother copied it down: "Delighted to know you exist. Thought I was the last Karlsevne on earth. Will arrive Friday night SAS at 11:40. Cousin Torfinn."

My mother sat with her mouth open. "This is crazy," she said. "I'm about to have a baby; your father is in Saudi Arabia, and his cousin . . ." She stopped and blew out a deep breath.

". . . is coming here. He doesn't ask, doesn't leave a phone number . . ."

She sat a few minutes longer, then typically, tried to do something about the visitor. Stop him! She placed another call to Gudrid, and the female voice that answered spoke Swedish. "*Var so god*," she said. "Please." Five minutes passed before a male voice said, over thousands of miles, that Gudrid had taken the ferry to the mainland to ski for a week before going to America. The voice was heavily accented.

"Do you know Torfinn Karlsevne?" my mother asked.

I'd gone upstairs to listen on the other phone.

"I've heard of him," the man said warily, as if he didn't want to discuss Torfinn Karlsevne. That was puzzling.

"Does he have a phone number?"

There was a moment's pause, as if a family decision was being made. "No."

My mother thanked him and hung up. I went back downstairs. She was still by the phone. Angry now. "Wouldn't you know your father would be away when this happens."

As she proceeded to dial Riyadh, the capital of Saudi, I went back upstairs to listen and say hi to my dad. There was a time lapse of eleven hours between the California coast and Riyadh, so it would be about five A.M., Thursday, where he was.

Awakened from a deep sleep, he sounded groggy, but my mother ignored that state to tell him she didn't appreciate his unknown cousin's visit; that he better find some way to get in touch with his cousin and make him delay his trip until after the baby was born. *Well* after!

I broke in to say, "Hi, Pop . . ."

"How yuh doin', Wendy?"

I said I was fine and looked forward to meeting Gudrid.

My mother and father talked for almost a half hour. Argued. Finally, he said, "Let him stay for two or three days, then tell him he has to go."

"Snorre, you don't know this man. He could be a thief, an addict, a rapist . . ."

"If his name is Karlsevne, he's a good man, Harriet. I've never heard anything bad about a Karlsevne . . ."

"Oh?" Her voice was full of gravel. "Well, that's reassuring. He's going to sleep here even if he might be a rapist. I'm going to cook for him. Should I make *frikadeller*? How about *hakkebiff*? How about me buying a bottle of *Taffel Akvavit*?" Akvavit was Scandinavian liquor.

"Come on, Harriet . . ."

My mother didn't say her usual "I love you" before hanging up.

Our old house, less than a hundred yards from the crashing California surf, had a New England smack about it, a stately Maine solidity. It fit in rather perfectly with the other vintage cottages, mostly weathered shingle.

All told, there were only five houses on that secluded stretch of Avesta Beach. It was sometimes dark and lonely during the gray fall and winter months. But my father liked it that way, though my mother didn't. Born in Minnesota, his Scandinavian blood demanded a slice of the old country coast. Avesta Beach, with its guano-whitened rocks and leisurely beds of kelp, often had the misty moods of *fjords*. It was, truly, a place for Vikings.

About six-thirty two nights later, there was a heavy rap on the front door. Visitors were few after sundown, and I looked at my mother and she looked back at me, frowning at the door, eyes narrowing.

"See who it is, Wendy," she said. Our visitor was not due until the following morning. It takes a while to get from San Francisco to Avesta.

I opened the door, and standing there was a man of about fifty, I estimated. He had a robust red beard. He was a huge man, dressed in a blue flannel shirt, brown corduroy pants of European cut, red kerchief around his thick neck. A black leather jacket encased his big shoulders. His hair was red-brown curling around his ears. Cousin Torfinn, of course, eyes of Baltic blue.

The big man grinned broadly, looking around and behind us. My mother had joined me. "Where is Cousin Snorre?"

"In Saudi Arabia," my mother said bleakly.

"What's he doing there?"

Torfinn spoke with the slightest chamois rub of Norselander. "He's a missile defense expert. How did you get here? Your plane isn't due until 11:40 tonight."

"It was early. I took a bus."

My mother nodded, but I saw suspicion as she glanced at me. The only bus going near Avesta passed at about three-thirty P.M. daily. "I'm Harriet, and this is our daughter Wendy."

Torfinn said quaintly, and with great charm, "You're a beautiful woman and with child."

Mother laughed nervously. "Yes, with child."

"How soon?"

"Three weeks or so."

"It will be a boy, a strong boy, a handsome boy," Cousin Torfinn said confidently.

"Perhaps," Mother said, allowing a smile. I could see that she was beginning to succumb to the winter-sky-blue eyes and the ivory grin of my father's cousin. Torfinn was at least six feet four and had the most powerful hands I'd ever seen.

Mother said, "Well, take off your coat and Wendy will show you to your room." His belongings were in an old canvas seabag.

Downstairs again, I went into the kitchen. Mother was by the stove. We were having soup that night. There was no problem in setting another bowl.

"Check SAS for me," she said, stirring the soup. She was still a little suspicious.

Just then, Torfinn clumped down the stairs and we walked back into the living room. He went to the beach-facing window. "I knew you'd live by the sea. It's in Snorre's blood. He'll sail eternally. Viking blood he's got. The tide goes in and out of his body."

"I suppose so," my mother said. "I'll put dinner on."

I said, "Let me show you something, Cousin Torfinn." I steered him into my father's library–home office. There were shelves of Viking books, models of longships; Viking shields and swords.

"It was a great age," he said approvingly. "History has never given us Vikings our just place." *Our!*

There was an old map on one wall. He said, "At one time we had Iceland, the Faroe, Norway, Sweden, Denmark, England, France, Holland, Scotland . . ."

He tapped a big finger at Gairsey, near the Pentland Firth, on the Scottish coast. "Sweyn Asliefssen used to come here. In the summer evenings you could hear the grind of swords and axes over ten hills and valleys."

I noticed Mother in the doorway, listening; amused.

During dinner, Torfinn talked about Thor, Ottar, and Leif Ericsson. About Halfdan Longlegs and Ragnar Hairybreeks and Harald Bluetooth. Told stories about them. "Ah, they were mighty men."

He was wonderful, and I knew Dad would love to hear him. How could I hang on to his cousin for another ten days?

"My father was Magnus Karlsevne and he traced our immediate family back to A.D. 605."

My mother murmured, "That's a long time back."

Torfinn nodded. "Now, the baby. You'll name him Snorre, of course."

"I doubt that very much. I prefer Michael or Mark," she answered crisply.

Frowning, he said, "Shame!" Then he repeated angrily, "Shame!"

My mother remained silent.

"You *will* name him Snorre!" His eyes were fierce.

My mother said, calmly, "We will name him what we choose to name him, or her, Cousin Torfinn."

The big man glared at her and finished his meal in silence, then said, "I'd like to take a walk. Do you mind?"

"Not at all," Mother said.

As soon as the door closed, none too gently, behind him, Mother said to me, "Call SAS. I want to know exactly when he arrived."

I did as told. The lady at SAS said, "Sorry, no passenger by that name on last night's flight."

I went back to the kitchen and lied. "He came in last night." I didn't want to see him kicked out before Dad came home. I believed that my mother would warm to Cousin Torfinn in a day or two. But I also wondered how he'd gotten here so quickly. He didn't look like a man who'd take a taxi all the way from San Francisco.

We went up to bed, and I think Mother fell asleep right away. With the baby banging around inside her, she caught sleep when she could.

I stayed awake, thinking about our visitor, and SAS and my lie, and then over the moaning wind I heard a voice. I got up and went to the window. Mr. Kelly, our next-door neighbor, was below. He shouted again. "Snorre, I've got to talk to you . . ."

"Daddy isn't here. I'll come down." I slipped on a robe.

Old Kelly was on the porch with a rifle in his hands. A small, wizened man of about seventy, he had large bloodshot eyes and skin the color of tallow. He was half deaf and couldn't see very well.

"Where's your pa?" he rasped.

"In Saudi Arabia."

"That's just great." In the soft light of the porch, I could tell he was frightened. "I just killed a man on the beach."

"You did *what*?" I could barely speak.

"I saw a man go by my place, a stranger. You know I don't like strangers. So I got my gun and followed him. I found him up by the rocks grinding an axe against them. I yelled at him, but he paid no attention. Then all of a sudden he turned and I saw the blade of the axe . . ."

Mr. Kelly stopped and took a deep breath. "I fired."

"Oh, my God," I said. "What did he look like?"

"A big, ugly brute with a red beard."

My heart slammed. "Stay here, Mr. Kelly. I'll get dressed."

Now it's time for YOU to be the Reader as Detective.

Whom did Mr. Kelly kill? How will Wendy respond? What will happen next?

Keep reading to find out!

I quickly pulled on jeans, a sweatshirt, and tennies* and took off, grabbing a flashlight. *Cousin Torfinn shot?*

With Mr. Kelly I hurried over the sand toward the outcropping about a quarter mile north, heart thumping, mouth dry.

---

*tennies: tennis sneakers

We got to the rocks and Mr. Kelly said, "Shine it over there." There was no body draining blood.

"Well, I'll be double-damned. He's not here."

"Are you sure you shot him? Did you see him fall?"

Mr. Kelly laughed sourly. "No, I panicked, Wendy. I ran! What did you expect me to do? But I tell you I shot a prowler out here twenty minutes ago. I'm old, but not crazy."

I looked around and shouted, "Torfinn! Cousin Torfinn!"

The only answer was the crash of surf; the moan of the damp salted wind.

"Who are you calling?" Mr. Kelly asked.

"My dad's cousin. He arrived here tonight from Sweden."

"Big fellow with a beard?"

"Yes."

Mr. Kelly suddenly became enraged. "What the devil was he doing with an axe?"

"I don't know," I answered weakly. My knees felt like melting butter. "But I'll try to find out. I'm glad you missed him."

Mr. Kelly grumbled. "Yeah. Tell him he got lucky."

A glazed half-moon was lodged in the sky, high over the fog bank that lay offshore. Faintly, over the south-blowing breeze, I could hear a joyful singsong baritone:

And then there was Torfinn
Who dealt a mighty blow
And chopped off the head of
The Merry Earl of Stoe . . .

I shivered, thankful Mr. Kelly couldn't hear it, and said to him, "We might as well go home."

"My rheumatism agrees."

We walked back to the five houses and I said good night to old Kelly.

"Tell him to stay off the beach at night if he wants to live," he advised.

"I will," I said. Then I added, "Please don't say anything to my mother about this. With the baby due, she's already nervous."

"All right," he grumbled and went on into his house.

I went into our house and into my father's "Viking" room and took Sorenson's *Viking Years*, the most accurate of all his reference books, off the shelf. I read: ". . . after killing Thangbrand and

Thorvald, Thorfinn's last conquest before setting sail for Hudson Bay was the beheading of the Earl of Stoe. It is a matter of record that he killed eleven men, but records of that period are conservative and one may safely count at least twenty heads that fell victim to Thorfinn's wrath with his sword and axe."

I sat there a while thinking about Cousin Torfinn. He certainly wasn't a ghost. I could stick my finger in his chest and it would hit flesh. But that fiendish song bothered me.

In bed again, I tossed and turned, waiting to hear Torfinn's heavy feet on the stairs. But I finally fell asleep, thinking about the "body" Mr. Kelly thought he saw; thinking about my SAS lie.

Be a Reading Detective

Read each of the following questions. Then write the letter of the correct answer to each question. Remember, the symbol next to each question identifies the *kind* of reading skill that particular question helps you to develop.

1. This part of the story is mainly about

   a. Wendy's father being in Saudi Arabia.
   b. the family hiring a nursemaid.
   c. the history of the Vikings.
   d. a strange cousin coming to visit.

2. First Wendy liked Gudrid because she sounded nice on the phone. Wendy's next reason for liking her was that she

   a. knew Gudrid would be a big help with the baby.
   b. looked forward to meeting somebody who was her cousin.
   c. thought it would be fun to hang around with Gudrid.
   d. knew that Gudrid would have good personal recommendations.

3. Which of these happened first?

a. They set a date for Gudrid to arrive.

b. Wendy's mother got a cablegram.

c. Wendy said hi to her father in Riyadh.

d. Wendy's mother tried to stop Cousin Torfinn.

4. What feature do Wendy's father and Cousin Torfinn have in common?

a. a bushy beard

b. blue eyes

c. red hair

d. broad shoulders

5. "Awakened from a deep sleep, he sounded groggy, but my mother ignored that state to tell him she didn't appreciate his unknown cousin's visit . . ." Another word for *groggy* here is

a. angry.

b. weird.

c. sleepy.

d. surprised.

6. Read these sentences said by Wendy's mother to her father.

"'Oh?' Her voice was full of gravel. 'Well, that's reassuring. He's going to sleep here even if he might be a rapist. I'm going to cook for him. Should I make *frikadeller*? How about *hakkebiff*?'"

What important point is the writer is trying to make here?

a. The family is descended from the Vikings.

b. Wendy's mother is angry.

c. The family doesn't know this cousin.

d. Wendy's father wants his cousin to be comfortable.

7. Which statement from the story is *not* a fact?

   a. "In the ad, my father had requested that the nursemaid be named Karlsevne."
   b. "My mother and father talked for almost a half hour."
   c. "Sorry, no passenger by that name on last night's flight."
   d. "It will be a boy, a strong boy, a handsome boy . . ."

8. Mr. Kelly is not sure if he really shot somebody because he

   a. got scared and ran away.
   b. didn't hear anybody cry out.
   c. doesn't have very good aim.
   d. is confused by the loud sea.

9. Why does Wendy shiver on page 249?

   a. It is cold and dark outside.
   b. She forgot to put on a pair of shoes.
   c. She's glad Cousin Torfinn is alive.
   d. The song she hears makes her uneasy.

10. By the end of this section of the story, how does Wendy feel about Cousin Torfinn?

    a. suspicious
    b. excited
    c. relieved
    d. curious

Follow the Trail

Setting

Remember that the **setting** of a story is where and when the story occurs. Answer the following questions about the setting in "The Grind of an Axe."

11. This story takes place in
    a. Bornholm, Sweden.
    b. San Francisco, California.
    c. Riyadh, Saudi Arabia.
    d. Avesta Beach, California.

12. Why might the author have chosen to have this story take place near the ocean?
    a. It gives Cousin Torfinn a place to walk at night.
    b. It relates well to Viking history and geography.
    c. It helps to make the house feel like a vacation spot.
    d. It shows how far Sweden is from San Francisco.

13. From Wendy's description on page 245, it is clear that the beach and house are
    a. isolated.
    b. new.
    c. bright.
    d. scary.

14. The story most likely occurs
    a. in modern times.
    b. in the future.
    c. in the 1950s.
    d. when the Vikings first came to America.

15. Where does Mr. Kelly say that he shot Torfinn?
    a. outside Wendy's window
    b. in front of Wendy's house
    c. by his porch
    d. a quarter of a mile away

Find Word Meanings

The five words listed on the next page appear in the first part of "The Grind of an Axe." Study the words and their definitions. Use the page numbers to check how the words are used in the story. Then complete the following sentences by using each vocabulary word only *once*.

word	meaning	page
impaling	piercing or running through the body	243
typically	expectedly; just as one would normally do	244
quaintly	in an old-fashioned, but still appealing, way	246
succumb	give in; give up	246
wizened	old; shriveled	248

In Part 1 of "The Grind of an Axe," we meet the main characters. Wendy is the sixteen-year-old narrator who gets swept up in the excitement of having a visitor. Wendy's dad is a Viking who is very proud of his heritage and likes to talk to his daughter about his past. When he tells her about Viking history, he looks at her with piercing, _____16_____ eyes to command her attention. He feels a bond with all people of his descent, and he wants to extend the same welcome to Torfinn that they'd _____17_____ extend to any other friend or family.

Harriet is Wendy's mom. She's more skeptical about having a stranger stay with them, but we eventually see her _____18_____ to the pressure to let him stay.

The neighbor, Kelly, is a _____19_____ old man.

Cousin Torfinn is a big, loud man, but sometimes he can be gentle and speak politely and _____20_____.

Look at Language

Context Clues

As you've learned, *context* refers to the words and sentences around a specific word. The context of a word can help you to figure out the meaning of an unfamiliar word.

These questions about words in the first part of "The Grind of an Axe" will give you practice using context clues.

21. Based on the context in the fourth paragraph (page 242), what is most likely the meaning of the word *estimated*?

    a. dreaded
    b. unexpected
    c. faked
    d. predicted

22. Which is another word to use for *enraged* on page 249?

    a. furious
    b. confused
    c. embarrassed
    d. disappointed

23. "I sat there a while thinking about Cousin Torfinn. He certainly wasn't a ghost. I could stick my finger in his chest and it would hit flesh. But that fiendish song bothered me." *Fiendish* probably means

    a. calming.
    b. evil.
    c. depressing.
    d. friendly.

24. "A black leather jacket encased his big shoulders. His hair was red-brown curling around his ears. Cousin Torfinn, of course, eyes of Baltic blue." A synonym for *encased* is

    a. enclosed.
    b. draped.
    c. stretched.
    d. puffed.

25. "'I've heard of him,' the man said warily, as if he didn't want to discuss Torfinn Karlsevne. That was puzzling." *Warily* means

    a. warmly.
    b. cautiously.
    c. amusingly.
    d. frighteningly.

Review the Case

The following activities will help you review and reflect on what happened in "The Grind of an Axe," Part 1.

1. Discuss. Cousin Torfinn gets very angry about what the baby will be named. What do you think of his outburst at the dinner table? Explain.

2. Write. Imagine you are applying for the nursemaid job at Wendy's house. Prepare an e-mail for Wendy's mother and father to convince them to hire you. Make sure that you are approachable but also professional, and that you list the experiences you have that qualify you for the job (if you don't have any experience, you can make some up for the sake of this activity).

3. Technology Application. Viking history plays an important role in this story. Conduct online research and find out about the Vikings. Who were they? Where and when did they live? What are they known for? Write a paragraph outlining your findings.

"Then I will stay longer and deal with your father," he said flatly. It sounded like a threat.

The Grind of an Axe

PART 2

In the morning, Torfinn was already in the kitchen when I went downstairs. Coffee was on. He'd made himself at home. I said, "You see anyone on the beach last night during your walk?"

"Not a soul. I owned the sand and stars. It was glorious."

"Our neighbor said he saw a man grinding an axe up by the rocks. He said the man was big and had a beard."

Torfinn smiled. "Hmmmmmm . . ." The smile said more than words.

I said, innocently, "I still can't figure out how you got here so early yesterday when your plane wasn't due until almost midnight."

He kept smiling. "Oh, I cabled you the wrong date. I arrived night before last, slept at the airport, took a bus south yesterday; then walked in from the highway . . ."

That all seemed to check out, even though SAS said he wasn't listed. But airlines do make mistakes. And it would have taken him three hours to walk in from 101. I almost felt ashamed at having doubted him. Actually, it was my mother who was suspicious.

Just then she waddled in. "Good morning."

Torfinn grinned back. "*God morgon.*"

"Did you have a nice walk last night?" she asked.

"Ah, it was glorious. The tide was beginning to rush the way it does in The Skaw."

"I'm glad," she said and went about fixing breakfast. She seemed rested and relaxed.

I went out to get the newspaper and saw our axe by the corner of the garage. It was freshly sharpened and polished. *So he was by the rocks last night!* Old Kelly had missed.

When I went inside, Torfinn was on the phone talking to my father in Swedish. Now and then Torfinn would laugh heartily. They were having a good time. Mother and I felt out of it. I helped her with the dishes, wondering about Kelly and his rifle. Goofy old man.

Finally, Torfinn got off the phone and handed it to my mother. Immediately, she said, "I'll take it upstairs."

Torfinn nodded and said, "I have a job to do outside."

What job? I had my own to do, straightening my room, always a weekend chore.

Soon, Mother came in. She said, angrily, "Your father didn't ask his cousin to leave. He'll come home next Saturday. Meanwhile, he said if I wanted Torfinn to go, just ask him. He hoped I wouldn't." She sighed deeply and sat down on the edge of my bed. "It's just bad timing." Then she grunted. The baby had drop-kicked her.

About an hour later, I went downstairs and then out to the backyard. Wood chips were flying from the axe blade. I asked Torfinn what he was doing.

"Building a cradle for Snorre, the seventy-ninth."

Dad's hobby was woodworking. He had power tools and wood in a shed behind the garage. Torfinn had taken some white pine from the bin. "This cradle will not have a single piece of iron in it. I'll put it together with pegs, the way Vikings did theirs."

I called Mother out of the house to view the handiwork. She looked at it and said, "Torfinn, I received a beautiful bassinet at a shower two weeks ago. The baby will sleep in it."

He looked hurt, even angry, again. "You wait! This will be the most beautiful cradle you've ever seen."

She nodded, rolled her eyes, and returned inside.

I stayed out there awhile and watched him work, asking about Harald Bluetooth and Ragnar Hairybreeks and Kalf Scurvy and Jon Limpleg and Thorir Treebeard.

He finished the cradle in late afternoon and came into the house to say, "Now we must dedicate it."

Returning outside, my mother was impressed. "It's exquisite. You did all that with an axe?"

"Of course," he answered. "Now, I will take it to the sea and dip it. You will witness."

We looked at the towering redheaded man. His hands were like giant clamshells. Mother agreed meekly.

Soon, we stood at water's edge, where foam lay in sudsy coils. Torfinn waded in over his boots and gently placed the *krubba* in the sea, talking to it, first in Swedish, then in English: "The sea will swell your seams and fill you with strength; the child that rests within your arms will someday return to The Skaw and Pentland Firth . . ."

My mother had tears in her eyes at the simple unforgettable charm of the ceremony.

I discovered Mr. Kelly's body halfway between the house and the rocks. I'd gone to his house to tell him that Cousin Torfinn was a very nice man. After all, he'd built a cradle for the baby. Mr. Kelly wasn't home, and I went out looking for him. He often surf-fished in late afternoon.

About two hours after his body was taken off to the mortuary, I sat in the front room with my mother and a uniformed officer. He'd already talked briefly to Cousin Torfinn. Finally, the officer said, "An autopsy will tell us what happened." We'd told him about Mr. Kelly's heart condition.

"He was a wonderful old man," my mother said. "We'll miss him."

After the officer departed, I went out to the tool room where Torfinn was painting flower designs on the head and sides of the cradle. I said, "Did you see our neighbor on the beach today?"

"Yes."

"Did you talk to him today?"

Torfinn nodded.

"How did he look?"

"He looked very ill the last time I saw him."

After dinner I went to the front porch where Torfinn was sitting. He looked over and said, poetically, "The waves are fighting each other tonight. There's a storm somewhere, far off. In the other ocean I could tell you where. Maybe off the Faroe, or as far away

as the Azores. I can tell by the sound of the sea, and the taste of the wind."

Maybe he was a real Viking, a ghost of the man who discovered America. Maybe he was both living and dead.

Sitting beside him I watched the surf for a long time, the long white lines advancing in the darkness, then I said, "Cousin Torfinn, what happened to Harry Kelly today?"

He deliberated a moment, then said, "You are family and dear to me. I would not lie to you. He died of fright."

Horrified, I asked, "You frightened him to death?"

He laughed curiously. "Me? Heaven forbid. No, no. If it happened, it was accidental."

"What did happen?"

"I was half asleep in the sun on the beach, with my eyes closed, and I heard someone coming. I felt them bending over. I could feel breath in my face. I suddenly opened my eyes and shouted, 'Boo.' The poor man keeled over."

"Why didn't you tell us? Why did you leave him there? Why didn't you tell the officer when he questioned you?"

He frowned at me in amazement. "I'm a visitor here. I'm an alien. It would not go well."

Mr. Kelly was dead, and he was responsible. Yet it didn't bother him. I said, "You must leave. It isn't working out the way I planned. Now, we have to tell the police."

"What good would that do? Do you try a man in court for saying 'Boo'?"

"I have to tell my mother," I said.

He said, slowly, but with determination, "Your brother must be Snorre. You must order your mother to do that. And I must be the godfather. After he is born and christened, I will go. I did not mean to cause you trouble."

In despair, I said, "This isn't the old country, Cousin Torfinn. No one can order my mother to do anything."

The bearded man looked off at the white hilltops of sea. "Then I will stay longer and deal with your father," he said flatly. It sounded like a threat.

So that I wouldn't upset my mother, I decided to wait until Dad returned Saturday to tell him about everything that had happened. Then he could deal with it.

But something else had happened. Mother had changed her mind about Cousin Torfinn. She said to me, "I guess I'm just a nutty female 'with child,' as he said." She admitted she was beginning to understand how he felt about having a family name for the newborn. She would now agree to Snorre, Jr.

I stood there openmouthed. She'd argued with my father over my name. He'd wanted Piger or Jenter or Flickor and she'd absolutely refused. Now, she was going to accept Snorre, Jr. Cousin Torfinn had bewitched her. I couldn't believe it.

I said, "Are you sure?"

She nodded, almost teary-eyed. I guess pregnant women become emotional in their last weeks.

The next day when Torfinn was out of the house, I did a sneaky thing. I looked around his room. There was a half-empty bottle of *akvavit* and he'd taken one of Dad's broadswords. I guess he was polishing it, maybe sharpening it. Steel wool and linseed oil were beside it on the table. The blade gleamed.

Late that same evening, while he was on another of his long beach walks, there was a rap on the front door. I opened it and a tall girl stood there. A Yellow Cab from Watsonville was at the end of our walk. The girl was not beautiful. She was quite plain. Oddly enough, on her face was fright.

Now it's time for YOU to be the Reader as Detective.

Who is this girl, and why is she on Wendy's doorstep? Why does she look scared?

Finish the story to find out if you're right.

Her first words were, "My name is Gudrid Karlsevne. I'm from Bornholm . . ."

I started to say, "Welcome," but her second words spilled out.

"Is my Uncle Torfinn here?"

"Yes," I said. "He's walking the beach."

"Do you have an axe?" Her eyes were wide.

"Yes."

"Where is it?"

"By the woodpile."

"Is it there now?"

"It was this afternoon."

"Look now."

We hurried to the rear of the garage. No axe.

Then words rushed out. Face chalky white, blue eyes big, hands trembling. Gudrid said, "He's insane. He escaped from Bornholm Hospital the evening after I visited him and told him I was coming to America to Cousin Snorre Karlsevne's house in California to be a nursemaid. I told him everything, without thinking. After he escaped, he went to his house, and got his passport, got money he'd hidden before the murder trial. None of my family ever thought he'd come here. They thought he'd gone to Norway or Denmark. So did I. But then on the plane coming here, I thought, 'Could he have gone to your house?' I'm so sorry. He's very clever. He has that terrible disease, one minute kind and gentle; the next he'll kill you if you make him angry . . ."

As she was saying all of that, the cold edge of the wind carried a singsong baritone:

And then there was Torfinn
Who dealt a mighty blow
And chopped off the head of
The Merry Earl of Stoe . . .

I ran to call 911.

Be a Reading Detective

Read each of the following questions. Then write the letter of the correct answer to each question. Remember, the symbol next to each question identifies the *kind* of reading skill that particular question helps you to develop.

1. How does Wendy know that Cousin Torfinn was out by the rocks where Mr. Kelly said he saw him?

    a. She hears him tell her father about it.
    b. Her mother says she heard him singing.
    c. Cousin Torfinn tells her he was there.
    d. She sees that their axe has been sharpened.

2. When Wendy says her mother was *impressed* on page 259, she means that her mother

    a. was angry with Cousin Torfinn.
    b. thought the cradle was well made.
    c. didn't want to use the cradle.
    d. felt that Cousin Torfinn was strange.

3. Read this paragraph from the story.

"I stood there openmouthed. She'd argued with my father over my name. He'd wanted Piger or Jenter or Flickor and she'd absolutely refused. Now, she was going to accept Snorre, Jr. Cousin Torfinn had bewitched her. I couldn't believe it."

What is the main point of this paragraph?

    a. Wendy is surprised at her mother.
    b. The baby's name will be Snorre, Jr.
    c. Wendy wishes she had a different name.
    d. Wendy's parents argue a lot.

4. "After the officer departed, I went out to the tool room where Torfinn was painting flower designs on the head and sides of the cradle." Another way to say *departed* is

    a. finished.
    b. agreed.
    c. left.
    d. answered.

5. Which happened first?

a. Cousin Torfinn built a cradle.
b. Harriet agreed to name the baby Snorre, Jr.
c. Wendy saw the axe sharpened and polished.
d. Wendy looked for Mr. Kelly on the beach.

6. What reason does Cousin Torfinn give for not telling the police officer that he scared Mr. Kelly?

a. He says it doesn't matter.
b. He says he is an outsider.
c. He says he is afraid.
d. He says he wants to christen the baby.

7. Wendy tells Cousin Torfinn he should leave after

a. she finds out he was responsible for Mr. Kelly's death.
b. he builds a cradle for the baby.
c. Gudrid tells Wendy that Torfinn is crazy.
d. Cousin Torfinn makes her mother cry.

8. The song Cousin Torfinn sings describes events in history, but it also

a. has a beautiful, unforgettable melody.
b. is a lullaby for the new baby.
c. makes you think about the Vikings.
d. helps you imagine what he might do.

9. Which is a fact about the story?

a. Torfinn is a really scary person.
b. Wendy's mom is kind to Torfinn.
c. Torfinn escaped from a hospital.
d. Wendy is too trusting of Torfinn.

10. If this part of the story were a newspaper article, the best title would be

a. "Old Man Frightened to Death."
b. "Dangerous Man Escapes from Asylum."
c. "Stranger Sings on Local Beach."
d. "Family Hires Suspicious Nursemaid."

Follow the Trail

Mood

Remember that **mood** is the feeling a story creates in a reader. Answer the following questions about mood in the second part of "The Grind of an Axe."

11. "I went out to get the newspaper and saw our axe by the corner of the garage. It was freshly sharpened and polished. *So he was by the rocks last night*! Old Kelly had missed." What mood is the author trying to create here?

    a. fun
    b. anxious
    c. subdued
    d. dreamy

12. Which best describes the mood created by Wendy on page 260?

    a. content
    b. passionate
    c. hopeless
    d. suspicious

13. Why does the author include details about Torfinn sharpening the axe and sword?

    a. to connect Torfinn to Viking history
    b. to create a feeling of fear
    c. to show Torfinn is good with his hands
    d. to help Wendy figure out Mr. Kelly's death

14. Which sentence BEST adds to the feeling of suspense at the end of the story?

    a. "Cousin Torfinn had bewitched her."
    b. " 'He's walking the beach.' "
    c. " 'He has that terrible disease . . .' "
    d. "We hurried to the rear of the garage."

15. What sort of mood does Torfinn's song give to the end of the story?

 a. gentle
 b. sad
 c. cheerful
 d. eerie

Find Word Meanings

The five words listed below appear in the second part of "The Grind of an Axe." Study the words and their definitions. Use the page numbers to check how the words are used in the story. Then complete the following sentences by using each vocabulary word only *once*.

word	meaning	page
heartily	with energy and cheerfulness	258
dedicate	to devote to, or set aside for a special purpose	259
exquisite	especially beautiful	259
mortuary	a place where dead bodies are stored and prepared for funerals	259
deliberated	thought about at length, tried to make a decision about	260

Part 2 of "The Grind of an Axe" kept me at the edge of my seat. Sometimes Torfinn seemed nice, and other times he seemed really creepy. When Torfinn laughed fully and _____16_____, he seemed like a happy person. And when Torfinn made a gorgeous, _____17_____ cradle and wanted to _____18_____ it to the baby by dipping it into the sea, he seemed to be very good-natured. But it seemed like there was another side to him, too. For example, he became angry at the smallest things, and he didn't seem to care that Kelly was dead and was taken to the _____19_____. I _____20_____ about whether Torfinn had killed Kelly, or whether it was just a coincidence. But once his niece arrived and said that Torfinn had escaped from a hospital, I knew that he was guilty!

Look at Language

Verb-Adverb Pairs

As you've learned, **verbs** lend strong action to stories and **adverbs** can help to describe events in vivid detail. Go back to the "Look at Language" sections on verbs (page 130) and adverbs (page 139) to refresh your memory. Then answer these questions about "The Grind of an Axe," Part 2.

21. "We looked at the towering redheaded man. His hands were like clamshells. Mother agreed meekly." The verb-adverb pair "agreed meekly" tells you that Wendy's mother

   a. was enthusiastic.
   b. felt weak compared to this big man.
   c. was only pretending to agree.
   d. was too angry to argue.

22. "He laughed curiously. 'Me? Heaven forbid. No, no. If it happened, it was accidental.'" *Laughed curiously* tells you he was acting

   a. warm and genuine.
   b. a bit strange and suspicious.
   c. sarcastic and unkind.
   d. puzzled and confused.

23. "He looked over and said, poetically, 'The waves are fighting each other tonight.'" *Poetically* modifies (describes) what word?

   a. looked
   b. said
   c. he
   d. waves

24. "About two hours after his body was taken off to the mortuary, I sat in the front room with my mother and a uniformed officer. He'd already talked briefly to Cousin Torfinn." Which is an adverb-verb pair?

   a. front room
   b. talked briefly
   c. uniformed officer
   d. was taken

25. "Now and then Torfinn would laugh heartily." You learned the word *heartily* in "Finding Word Meanings" on page 266. What does this mean about how he laughed?

   a. sarcastically
   b. cruelly
   c. warmly
   d. deeply

Review the Case

The following activities will help you review and reflect on what happened in "The Grind of an Axe," Part 2.

1. **Discuss.** Cousin Torfinn makes Wendy's baby brother or sister a cradle. He also has another angry outburst. Explain how you reacted to his making the cradle and to his insistence that Wendy's mother use it.

2. **Write.** The story ends with Wendy calling 911. What do you think happens next? Write a continuation of the story for two or three more paragraphs.

3. **Technology Application.** Choose a main character from either half of the story. If that character had a page on a social-networking site like Facebook or MySpace, what would be on the page? Write a brief description of the page. Who would be that character's friends? What would be his or her quote or status? What groups would he or she like?

Glossary

A

accurate without errors; correct
active lively; showing much attention
alert wide-awake; very watchful
ammunition items that are used in attacking or defending something or someone
array collection, assortment
assistance help
astounded greatly surprised

B

babbled chatted unintelligently, talked endlessly
beckoned motioned or gestured to come nearer
beneficiary the recipient of something good; somebody or something that gets money
bleachers benches or stands for the fans at sporting events
bragging praising or boasting about oneself
buckled folded, lost strength, gave way under

C

career life's work; way of living
caution warn
chill make cold; sudden coldness
coincidence the chance happening of two things in such a way as to be striking or unusual
commence begin, start to
companion one who shares in what another is doing
compete try to win something wanted by others
compounded piled up, put one on top of each other
conceal hide; keep secret
contrary going against, disagreeing with or disobeying
conveyed expressed or communicated

D

debilitating making something or someone unable to function properly
debris broken pieces, leftover bits of unwanted substances
dedicate to devote to, or set aside for a special purpose
deliberated thought about at length, tried to make a decision about

deliberately on purpose, intending to do
descended broken pieces, leftover bits of unwanted substances
despite even though
deterrent something that discourages somebody from doing
   something
disintegrated fell apart, broke down

E

elude avoid
entirely completely
exaggerating going beyond the truth
exceedingly very; greatly
exhumation removal of a body from a grave for examination
expressly specifically
exquisite especially beautiful

F

faculties mental powers or abilities
fascinating of great interest
fatal causing death or ruin
furnished supplied

G

genuflected bent knees or bowed down on one knee
gnarled curled up unnaturally, bent, twisted
granted given; awarded

H

hapless unlucky; lacking ability
heartily with energy and cheerfulness
hysterical highly excited; out of self-control

I

immensely extremely great in size or quality
impaling to pierce or run through the body
inflammation swelling, irritation
inspection the act of looking at closely
intelligence ability to learn and know
intent strong purpose; strongly fixed on something
introduction beginning or starting point; making known
investigation a careful search

K

keen sharp

L

lobby entrance hall

M

mortuary a place where dead bodies are stored and prepared for funerals

mustiness stuffiness, moldiness

O

observe see and note; study

obtaining getting

ominous scary; giving a feeling that something is happening or is about to happen

P

paratrooper a soldier who parachutes into enemy territory

pollution the dirtying of conditions that affect the growth of life

prevent stop; keep from happening

probable likely to happen; likely to be true

probing searching, exploring

provide offer up; supply

Q

quaintly in an old-fashioned, but still appealing, way

R

recollection memory

reflect think carefully

remarkable unusual

remedial meant to improve or correct

reputation good name; fame

resilient strong, able to recover quickly

romanticized made to seem larger than life, or more fanciful

S

satisfying pleasing; enjoyable

shudder shake with fear

shuffling walking with small steps, without lifting feet, dragging feet

slackening letting up, getting weaker

soothingly calmly; quietly
sore angry; upset
sparse not dense, thinly populated, bare
spellbound too interested to move
staggered tripped over, walked unsteadily
stagnant unmoving and dirty, stale
stashed hid
steady changing little; firm
stifle keep covered or unknown, push down
succumb give in, give up
sufficient enough, able to satisfy a need
supervise watch over, be in charge of
surged moved in a strong, sudden motion

T

tempered made less intense, toned down
tolerant understanding, putting up with
tragedy a terrible happening; unusual sadness
triumph success; victory
tumultuously in a disorganized way, randomly
typically expectedly, just as one would normally do

U

undisguised not hidden; open

V

vaguest slightest; very unclear
vast very great
vehicle any means of carrying, communicating, or making known
vibrant bright, lively and energetic
vivid lively; clear; distinct

W

withering attempting to cut down
wizened old, shriveled

Acknowledgments

Grateful acknowledgment is made to the following sources for permission to reprint copyrighted materials. Every effort has been made to obtain permission to use previously published material. Any errors or omissions are unintentional.

"The Adventure of the Speckled Band," by Sir Arthur Conan Doyle. Page 1.

"After Twenty Years," by O. Henry. From *The Four Million*, by O. Henry. Copyright © 1904 by Press Publishing Co. Reprinted by permission of Doubleday & Company, Inc. Page 41.

"Sarah Tops," by Isaac Asimov. © Copyright by Isaac Asimov. Reprinted by permission of the Estate of Isaac Asimov. Page 51.

"The Open Window," by Saki. From *The Complete Short Stories of Saki*, by Saki (H. H. Munro), edited by Christopher Morley. Copyright 1930, renewed © 1958 by The Viking Press, Inc. Page 61.

"One Throw," by W. C. Heinz. Reprinted by permission of William Morris Endeavor Entertainment, LLC, on behalf of the Estate of W. C. Heinz. Copyright © 1950, renewed 1978 by W. C. Heinz. Page 71.

"I've Got Gloria" by M. E. Kerr, copyright © 1997 by M. E. Kerr, from NO EASY ANSWERS: SHORT STORIES ABOUT TEENAGERS MAKING TOUGH CHOICES by Donald Gallo, editor. Used by permission of Delacorte Press, an imprint of Random House Children's Books, a division of Random House, Inc. (Note: Photo that appears with this story was not used in the original selection.) Page 83.

"Just Once" by Thomas J. Dygard, copyright © 1995 by Thomas Dygard, from ULTIMATE SPORTS by Donald R. Gallo. Used by permission of Random House Children's Books, a division of Random House, Inc. (Note: Photo that appears with this story was not used in the original selection.) Page 97.

"The Leopard Man's Story," by Jack London. Page 111.

"The Purloined Letter," by Edgar Allan Poe. Page 121.

Saferstein, FORENSIC SCIENCE AN INTRODUCTION NASTA ED, "Case Study—Joann Curley: Caught by a Hair" pp. 227–228, © 2008. Reproduced by permission of Pearson Education, Inc. Page 142.

"All Summer in a Day," by Ray Bradbury, is reprinted by permission of Don Congdon Associates, Inc. Copyright © 1954, renewed 1982 by Ray Bradbury. Page 153.

"The Treasure of Lemon Brown" by Walter Dean Myers. Reprinted by permission of Miriam Altshuler Literary Agency, on behalf of Walter Dean Myers. Copyright © 1983, by Walter Dean Myers. Page 167.

"Born Worker" from PETTY CRIMES: Stories by Gary Soto. Copyright © 1998 by Gary Soto. Reprinted by permission of Houghton Mifflin Harcourt Publishing Company. All rights reserved. Page 184.

"Born Worker" from *Petty Crimes* by Gary Soto. Text copyright © 1998 by Gary Soto. Used with permission of the author and BookStop Literary Agency. All rights reserved. Page 184.

"August Heat," from THE BEAST WITH FIVE FINGERS by William Fryer Harvey, copyright 1947 by E.P. Dutton & Co. Used by permission of Dutton, a division of Penguin Group (USA) Inc. Page 209.

"Every Fifth Man," by Edward D. Hoch. Originally appeared in *Ellery Queen's Mystery Magazine*, Copyright © 1968; reprinted by permission of the Author's Estate and the Sternig & Byrne Literary Agency. Page 221.

"On the Outlaw Trail," from *Talking Bones: The Science of Forensic Anthropology* by Peggy Thomas, published by Facts On File, Inc., 1995. Copyright © 1995 by Peggy Thomas. Reprinted with permission of Facts On File, Inc., an imprint of Infobase Publishing, Inc. Page 231.

"The Grind of the Axe," by Theodore Taylor. Reprinted by permission of the Theodore Taylor Estate and the Watkins/Loomis Agency. Page 242.

Photo and Art Credits

Godey's ladies fashions, 1890s. © North Wind Picture Archives. Page 3.

Single Diamond Isolated on White. © www.iStockphoto.com/ Evgeny Terentev. Page 41.

Dinosaur Skull. © www.iStockphoto.com/Josh Laverty. Page 53.

View from a Window. © www.iStockphoto.com/Dietmar Klement.

Up to Bat! (Baseball Vector) © www.iStockphoto.com/JSatt 83. Page 72.

Bulldog Lying on Floor. © www.iStockphoto.com/Iofoto. Page 84.

Failing Grade. © www.iStockphoto.com/Stacey Newman. Page 87.

Running Back. © www.iStockphoto.com/Brandon Laufenberg Page 98.

Microscope Silhouette. © www.iStockphoto.com/Fckuen. Page 124.

Beware Toxic. © www.iStockphoto.com/Alohaspirit. Page 142.

Green Leaf in a Sunny Day. © www.iStockphoto.com/Chaikovskiy Igor. Page 154.

Spring Foliage. © www.iStockphoto.com/Carlos Caetano. Page 157.

Boarded Up. © www.iStockphoto.com/Frank van der Bergh. Page 169.

The Old Harmonica. © www.iStockphoto.com/Jaime Roset. Page 175.

Wood Shingle Background. © www.iStockphoto.com/Douglas Allen. Page 186.

Empty Swimming Pool. © www.iStockphoto.com/Christopher Ingram. Page 189.

Loquats. © www.iStockphoto.com/Slallison. Page 197.

Dog. © www.iStockphoto.com/Ultramarinfoto. Page 200.

Tombstone. © www.iStockphoto.com/Jean Assell. Page 212.

Tree in Forest. © www.iStockphoto.com/Les Cunliffe. Page 221.

Battlements. © www.iStockphoto.com/Neal McClimon. Page 223.

Wanted Poster Wild West. © www.iStockphoto.com/Duncan Walker. Page 231.

Sheriff Badge - Isolated. © www.iStockphoto.com/SpxChrome. Page 234.

Swedish West Coast. © www.iStockphoto.com/Dirk Freder. Page 243.

Helmet, Sword, Axe, and Shield of Vikings. © www.iStockphoto.com/Stasyuk Stanislav. Page 247.

Baby Crib. © www.iStockphoto.com/Andy Gehrig. Page 260.

Index of Skills Taught In This Book

The six basic reading skills (see page iv) are covered after each story and are signaled in the text by their respective icons.

Finding the main idea
Identifying supporting details
Finding vocabulary clues

Putting events in sequence
Drawing inferences
Distinguishing fact from opinion

Additional reading skills covered

Vocabulary and language skills covered